REPRESENTING OTHERS: WHITE VIEWS OF INDIGENOUS PEOPLES

REPRESENTING OTHERS: WHITE VIEWS OF INDIGENOUS PEOPLES

Edited by Mick Gidley

UNIVERSITY
of
EXETER
PRESS
for AmCAS

Exeter Studies in American and Commonwealth Arts
Number 4

First published 1992
by the University of Exeter Press
Reed Hall
Streatham Drive
Exeter EX4 4QR

Reprinted 1994

British Library Cataloguing in Publication Data
Representing Others: White Views of
Indigenous Peoples.—(Exeter Studies in
American & Commonwealth Arts Series; No. 4)
    I. Gidley, M.   II. Series
305.8

ISBN 0–85989–354–5

Typeset in 10pt Plantin by
Kestrel Data, Exeter

Printed in Great Britain by
Short Run Press Ltd, Exeter

Contents

List of Illustrations   vii

Preface and Acknowledgements   ix

Mick Gidley   I
Representing Others: An Introduction

Stephanie Smiles   14
A Native American in Stone: The Simcoe Memorial in Exeter
Cathedral

Tim Youngs   25
The Medical Officer's Diary: Travel and Travail with the Self
in Africa

Anthony Fothergill   37
Of Conrad, Cannibals, and Kin

Ron Tamplin   60
Noble Men and Noble Savages

Peter Quartermaine   84
Johannes Lindt: Photographer of Australia and New Guinea

Mick Gidley   103
Edward S. Curtis' Indian Photographs: A National Enterprise

Richard Maltby   120
John Ford and the Indians; or, Tom Doniphon's History Lesson

Notes on Contributors   145

Index   147

List of Illustrations
(*between pages 84 and 85*)

1. Simcoe Memorial, Exeter Cathedral, by John Flaxman, 1815 (photograph, Allen J. Koppenhaver).

2. Townshend Memorial, Westminster Abbey, by Robert Adam, 1761 (by courtesy of the Warburg Institute, London).

3. Drawing by Flaxman in preparation for the Simcoe Memorial (by courtesy of the Victoria and Albert Museum, London).

4. 'The Commander in Chief of the Cherokees', c. 1762, anonymous engraving (by courtesy of the British Library, London).

5. Portrait of Joseph Brant, by George Romney, 1775-76, now in the National Gallery of Canada (by courtesy of the Witt Collection, Warburg Institute).

6. Native American figure in the Simcoe Memorial (photograph, Allen J. Koppenhaver).

7. Woodcut of Tupinamba Indians, probably by Johann Froschauer, 1505 (by courtesy of the Bayerische Staatsbibliothek, Munich).

8. 'English Church and Parsonage, Glenn Innis', photograph by Johannes Lindt, n.d. (by courtesy of National Library of Australia, Canberra).

9. Untitled photograph by Johannes Lindt from *Aboriginal Natives from Clarence River District*, 1875 (by courtesy of National Library of Australia, Canberra).

10. Untitled photograph by Johannes Lindt from *Aboriginal Natives from Clarence River District*, 1875 (by courtesy of National Library of Australia, Canberra).

11. 'Camped', photograph by Johannes Lindt, n.d. (by courtesy of the State Library of Victoria, Melbourne).

12. 'Near the Camp, Laloki River', photograph by Johannes Lindt, 1885 (by courtesy of National Library of Australia, Canberra).

13. 'Motu Water Carrier—Port Moresby', photograph by Johannes Lindt, 1885 (by courtesy of National Library of Australia, Canberra).

14. 'Native Teachers', photograph by Johannes Lindt, 1885 (by courtesy of National Library of Australia, Canberra).

15. 'Oasis in the Badlands', photogravure from a photograph by Edward S. Curtis, 1904 (by courtesy of Exeter University Library, Exeter).

16. 'Mosa—Mohave', photogravure from a photograph by Edward S. Curtis, 1903 (by courtesy of Exeter University Library).

17. 'Before the White Man Came—Palm Cañon', photogravure from a photograph by Edward S. Curtis, 1924 (by courtesy of Exeter University Library).

18. 'The Spirit of the Past—Apsaroke', photogravure from a photograph by Edward S. Curtis, 1906 (by courtesy of Exeter University Library).

Illustration No. 16 is also reproduced on the front cover of this book.

Preface and Acknowledgements

This book—both its conception and most of its content—arose out of the teaching experience of some of its contributors. In the early 1970s, at the urging of my then colleague Mike Weaver, I ran the first of a series of term-length 'cultures' projects in the University of Exeter undergraduate programme in American and Commonwealth Arts. We would study a specific American region (such as the West or the South), an ethnic group (say, Jewish-Americans, or Black Americans), or a definable time slot (perhaps the 1930s or the 1890s), using a range of materials—fiction, government documents, photographs, films, newspaper reports, etc. There was no pretence of completeness; these were probes, and there was much stress on students finding and consulting 'primary' resources and reporting back on what they had discovered. The projects were stimulating for the group as a whole, me included, and often led individual students into more developed research papers or dissertations in the chosen topic. Parallel projects emerged in the Commonwealth part of the programme, and the one Peter Quartermaine and Ronald Tamplin developed on the South Seas proved particularly successful.

All the while we talked informally about common questions of organisation, such as the appropriate balance of kinds of material, but it was not until the early 1980s that we realised sharply enough that the truly important issues of mutual concern were more conceptual, and much more intractable. (Some of the terms broached in these prefatory remarks, for example, such as 'culture', 'representation', 'white' or, even, 'indigenous', to give just four, are obviously complex, even fraught, and are so in ways not always taken up in this collection.) A little later —partly, ironically, as a result of government financial cuts—we regularised the core of the cultures aspect of our teaching into two repeatable units, the one on the South Seas already mentioned, and the other on the American West, taught by Richard Maltby and myself. In these projects the idea was to look at a variety of materials, both those produced by the respective indigenous peoples—whether material artefacts, such as carvings or baskets, mythologies (read in translation), songs, or literature composed in a variety of English—and those produced by visitors or settlers, predominantly white, from the relevant politically ascendant or already dominant power. We imagined that each student would develop from this collage of items an overall view of each region and its culture. As it happened, of course, the process was far more problematic and we often found ourselves discussing the *difficulties* of achieving a coherent view, sometimes with assistance from cultural theorists.

Since the other contributors to this volume, Anthony Fothergill, Stephanie Smiles and Tim Youngs, have neither been helped nor handicapped by debates within American and Commonwealth Arts, it is significant that they have found themselves not only pursuing similar problems, but being troubled by similar critical doubts. The present book is not so much an attempt to arrive at coherence as it is a further airing of some of the key issues. These are formulated with reference to bodies of material in a variety of media—from sculpture to the movies, from diaries and literary texts to photographs—that have most concerned us as individuals. We have chosen here to concentrate on white depictions of indigenous peoples. Needless to say, this is not through any lack of interest in indigenous creation. Also, we do not entertain the notion that the carvings or myths or, even, the musical rhythms of indigenous peoples could speak directly to members of different cultures, as it were, and it is planned that a future addition to this series of Exeter Studies in American & Commonwealth Arts will be devoted to such material. In considering the possible contents of the present book in the context of the manifest inequalities of our world, it seemed particularly pressing to try to understand something of the history of the relationship(s) between this lopsided distribution of economic and political power and the production and nature of white traveller's tales, films, etc. These essays, therefore, both instance examples of white depictions of indigenous peoples and cultures from the eighteenth century onwards and analyse some of the mechanisms employed by the dominant culture(s) in representing others. It is our implicit (and sometimes explicit) contention that it was partly through such representations that the colonising culture asserted its dominance.

Representing Others has been quite a time in the making, and those involved have all demonstrated remarkable forebearance. As editor, I have both accumulated extra debts and become ever more conscious of the helpfulness of my fellow workers at the University of Exeter. Efficient help with printed and audio-visual materials came from Julie

Crawley, Heather Eva and Nick Eastwood of the University Library. Supportive and cheerful secretarial assistance was provided by Patricia Dowse, Joanne Hill and Vi Palfrey of the School of English and American Studies. In planning the volume, contributions came from our former colleague in American and Commonwealth Arts, David Horn, as well as from present colleagues. I am very pleased to acknowledge all the work and suggestions of each of the contributors, but especially those of Richard Maltby, who is also General Editor of the book series in which it appears. In addition, ideas and information were offered by visiting professors Larry Owen and Margaret Szasz, by students taking the various Cultures courses and, coincident with (but definitely extra to) her role in word processing almost the entire contents, from Kate Bowles. The institutions which kindly provided prints and/or permissions for the illustrations are fully acknowledged by name in appropriate captions, but I would like to record my appreciation formally here; I am particularly grateful to Allen J. Koppenhaver, a former Fulbright professor at Exeter, for the use of his photographs of the Simcoe Memorial. Financial assistance towards publication was generously made available by the London office of the U.S. Information Service (Dr Ron Clifton, Cultural Attaché). Finally, and crucially, a Fellowship from the Netherlands Institute for Advanced Study enabled me to complete the task of editing the book.

Mick Gidley   Wassenaar, 1991

MICK GIDLEY

Representing Others: An Introduction

Edward S. Curtis, a figure who features in one of the studies in this volume, reported to a friend that after a performance in 1911 of his elaborate musicale or 'picture-opera' based on North American Indian culture—sometimes titled 'The Intimate Story of Indian Tribal Life'— Franklin Hooper, an eminent scientist of the time, Director of the Brooklyn Institute, told him that though 'they [at the Institute] had heard many phases of Indian life and seen fragments, . . . I was the first to give them . . . the real Indian; . . . he thought the entertainment a message of more than national importance. . . .' Obviously, what the audience at the Brooklyn Institute actually experienced was not 'the real Indian', to use Curtis' impossible formulation, or even what he himself as a photographer and ethnologist had witnessed in the field, but a representation.[1] Despite countless confusions to the contrary, it has been understood since the time of Aristotle that forms of cultural expression, both 'artistic' and otherwise—whether poetry or parliamentary records, songs or statistics, drawings or dramatic productions—do not reproduce reality itself; rather, in their various ways, these and other forms far too numerous to mention each offer something which *stands for* an aspect of reality.

The concept of representation, as a number of commentators have shown, is fundamental but also highly complex, especially in its relationship to ideas of 'realism', the sense that some forms, or individual examples within forms, offer better or, as is often said, closer approximations to reality than others.[2] Hence Hooper, confronted by Curtis' show—a show using lantern slides, movie footage, scenery (including a full-sized Plains tipi borrowed from the American Museum of Natural History), music and the spoken word in a more highly wrought manner than he had previously encountered—could be led, mistakenly, to believe he was getting the real thing. What such representations in fact offer are varying *illusions* of reality. Here I do not mean to imply 'mere illusions', to downgrade the significance of representations. For a start, they may be replete with skill or art, and, often for this reason, they may impress themselves with awesome force on those encountering them. The fact that representations are capable of exerting such power—and we know that some of those treated here have done so—is part of what makes them worth investigating.[3] Also, by referring to them as 'illusions', in no sense do I mean to suggest that they function only as symbols of something much more important, and lying behind them, as it were, in real life; rather, as the essays here help us to understand, these representations have in turn acted to *constitute* 'reality' for the cultures which produced and consumed them.[4]

Despite its apparent problems, the use of 'representation' as it has appeared so far does have certain advantages. One of them is that it may be enriched, if further complicated, by its association with the idea of political representation. That is, there is a relationship between what W.J.T. Mitchell calls 'things that stand for other things' and 'persons who act for other persons'. 'It should be clear', says Mitchell, 'that representation, even purely aesthetic representation of fictional persons and events, can never be completely divorced from political and ideological questions', and he points out that just as, for example, literature is often said to be a 'representation of life', it is to be expected that 'life' will affect the nature of the representation.[5] The essays in this volume instance and analyse exclusively representations produced by members of politically powerful—indeed, dominant—groups. In 'life' the subjects of these representations were also usually the political subjects of the producers' societies. It is a truism that to visitors in a new land—certainly to settlers—the original inhabitants were profoundly *Other*: the settlers may have had to struggle physically with the indigenous people for possession of the land, and in the process these original inhabitants were or became that which the settlers had to define themselves against. It was virtually inevitable that the representations examined here—though not always the products of settlers themselves, or even of the descendants of settlers—would incorporate, reflect or respond to, perhaps justify, the assumptions of the dominant. And, as we shall see, they do.

This view of the situation is a long way from simpler questions about the 'accuracy' or otherwise of a work's representation of the culture at issue. Indeed, in much recent thinking and writing on the representation of other cultures, often indebted to Edward W. Said's *Orientalism* (1978), his groundbreaking study of European scholarship, pronouncements (such as the speeches of politicians) and literature, including travellers' tales, devoted to the Middle East, a kind of consensus has emerged that members of the dominant group—no matter how 'intimate' (to use Curtis' word again) their sense of their involvement with the people concerned, no matter how deep their professed interest in their subject—will represent *nothing but* the assumptions of their own kind. Rather than seeking out or simply recognising the features held in common with the subject group, there will be a tendency, as James Clifford has put it, 'to dichotomize . . . into we-they contrasts and to *essentialize* the resultant other—to speak of the oriental mind, [etc]'. Thus we get the emergence of '*the* Arab', '*the* African', '*the* South Sea Islander', and so on, and on.[6] Instead of previously prevalent questions as to whether particular representations produced by white culture(s) depicted indigenous cultures with verisimilitude, it would seem that the appropriate question to ask today of one of white culture's products would be, What aspect of *itself* has it represented? Thus, a 1986 British Museum conference of museum curators predominantly from the western world and devoted primarily to anthropological exhibitions took as its very honest title 'Exhibiting Ourselves'.

And in this 'crisis of representation', as it has been called, what may be said about anthropology, the discipline within western learning usually seen as the one whose central business it was to describe and understand culture in general and other cultures in particular? The Mexican painter David Alfaro Siqueiros gave a suitably enigmatic title to his 1939 portrait, now in New York's Museum of Modern Art, of someone clothed in a Mexican peasant's smock, surrounded by darkness, and, crucially, wearing a decorative mask under a straw sombrero: 'Ethnography'. The picture is itself literally—or, rather, graphically—only a mask, a mystery hiding rather than revealing the nature of the life of the person and culture it represents. For a start, anthropologists themselves have bemoaned the degree to which, if sometimes unwittingly, the enterprise of their discipline was not immune to the influence of the kinds of inequalities we have noted but inextricably linked to the exercise of power by the dominant culture.[7] Also, in recent years attention has switched from the analysis of fieldwork in anthropology—what was collected, where, when, whether informants were likely to have known much about what they were saying, etc.—to scrutiny of the actual composition, the writing, of ethnographic texts. It was in the writing, after all, in the representation itself, that the subjects, 'others' and their cultures, were not so much even reconstructed as *constructed*. Looked at this way, it is clear that anthropologists tended to compose their accounts from a narrative point of

3

view which largely excluded signs of their own presence, which in turn made their ethnologies appear wholly coherent (even when incomplete), objective (if sympathetic), and above all, authoritative. The indigenous people and their cultures were fixed, so to speak, as if unchanging (and possibly unhangable), in what Johannes Fabian has analysed as 'the ethnographic present tense', which further accentuated their essential-isation.[8]

All round then, it probably cannot be emphasised enough that the representation—in any form of cultural expression—of any part of the social life of human beings is a complex business. Howard S. Becker, in his notably lucid and wide-ranging essay 'Telling about Society'—in which, incidentally, he professes a belief in the retention of some element of the real in the representation, as if by adhesion, while at the same time stressing that the representation 'leaves out much, in fact, *most*, of reality'—has reiterated some of the difficulties of these issues and pointed out that all representations involve what he summarises as processes of 'selection', 'translation', 'arrangement', and 'interpreta-tion'.[9] While the contributions to the present book do not concentrate on conceptual aspects of representation itself, they each explicitly or implicitly consider one or more of the categories of process that Becker has identified. Moreover, each medium—literary fiction, film, or whatever—is subject to its own different conventions in the way it represents reality. As we have observed, none of them are transparent windows, as it were. Each has its own codes, and the contributors to the present volume, as I shall underline below, have been sensitive to the operation of these in their chosen forms. Also, of course, the contributors employ the differing techniques of their varied disciplines—literary criticism, art history, history, etc.—while ultimately each of their contributions are essays in cultural history.

The contributions here proceed in roughly chronological order of their respective subject matter, from the early nineteenth century to almost our own immediate period, though with some slight adjustments for the sake of geographical coherence. It is particularly appropriate for a publication originating in Exeter that, as the topic to head off the book, Stephanie Smiles, herself of Native American descent, chose to treat John Flaxman's 1815 memorial to Colonel John Graves Simcoe, which, with its sculpted North American Indian figure, is to be found in Exeter Cathedral. She places the decision to include a Native American figure in a monumental sculpture within the tradition of such commemorative work, where from Roman times the figures of slaves or conquered peoples had appeared in, literally, supporting roles. As well as art history, she provides the figure with a rationale within the context of Indian-British relations in North America—and, indeed, in Britain—around the period when Simcoe was the first Governor of Upper Canada. In both art and life the Native American was generally, as she puts it, marginalised. At one and the same time, Flaxman's depiction of his figure was both a new and positive departure and at some level was also influenced by conceptions of one of the most persistent, indeed archetypal, representations of the Other, 'the noble savage'.[10]

In Tim Youngs' essay we move to another continent, Africa (though Australia also gets a significant mention), and to a different medium, the diary. Thomas Parke, medical officer to Henry Morton Stanley's controversial expedition to relieve Emin Pasha in the late 1880s, kept a diary which was published in 1891, fairly soon after his return to England. It is not simply the case that Youngs' reading of the diary puts a question mark over Stanley's mythic status as a hero once again, though it does do that. It is also clear from this account that far from being the relatively straightforward bearing of the individual soul or the purely internal dialogue it is sometimes assumed to be, the diary as a form is highly problematic, and this particular one certainly recorded a whole lot more than the personal and medical observations of its author. There were entries which touched upon well-documented points of conflict in Victorian culture, such as the nature of decorum, appropriate roles for women, and, of course, sexuality—topics which recur in other essays. We see that even Parke's graphic descriptions of ulcers, amputations, poisoning, the effects of fever and the like were not actually as 'scientific' as they purported to be. The ostensibly private diary supported the very public pursuits of empire.

The central topic of Anthony Fothergill's contribution, Joseph Conrad's short novel, *Heart of Darkness* (1899), is also set in late nineteenth century Africa, an era when colonialism was particularly aggressive, but his essay starts out with a reminder of the patterns of seeing first exhibited in European culture's much earlier encounter with the Indians of the New World. As might be expected, there have been a number of studies of literary representations of colonialism and related topics, but most of these have concentrated on the gung-ho jingoists or superseded adventure writers, like Rudyard Kipling, Rider Haggard and G. A. Henty, to name only British ones, and steered clear of figures as searching or as incontestably canonical as Conrad.[11] Anthony Fothergill demonstrates that representation of the Other in Conrad's novella—and in a Wordsworth poem—was marked by what he calls 'projection', 'contradiction', and 'negation', terms which could also be applied—and in certain cases are—to the characteristics of other representations featured in this book.

Ron Tamplin, in his study of aristocratic British travellers in the South Seas, contextualises his selected texts partly by an opening reference to Francis Galton's *The Art of Travel; or, Shifts and Contrivances Available in Wild Countries* (1855), an influential how-to book for writing travellers, as well as by frequent references to better known authorities on the region, such Robert Louis Stevenson and Jack London. He reveals, among other things, that sometimes his writers created South Sea islanders in the image of stereotypes derived from parallel treatments of Africans, and this explicit connection may serve as a reminder that one of the (largely unargued) assumptions behind this collection is that in the representation of indigenous peoples by the dominant culture(s) a similar pattern has persisted. At the same time, there were 'new' aspects to the representation of South Sea Islanders. Mark Twain, in hoping to publish a book 'constructed' by R.M. Daggett, a former US Minister to the Sandwich Islands, and 'the king of the Sandwich Islands, working together', said 'it is very curious—& *new*. It is fresh ground—untouched, unworn, & full of romantic interest'. That 'romantic interest', especially following Gauguin's Tahitian paintings of naked, beautiful women, as pickably 'available' as the flowers with which they adorned their hair, was frequently, as Ron Tamplin shows, sexually charged. In counterpoint to the pejorative associations with Africans, such representations of the islanders had a base in allusions to the classical age: they were, apparently, 'Greek bronzes come to life'. Perhaps we should take very *literally* the meaning of the title of Bernard Smith's seminal book on fine art depictions of the region: *European Vision and the South Pacific* (1960).[12]

'In the same quarter of the globe Australia is rising, or indeed may be said to have risen, into a grand centre of civilisation, which at some not very remote period', claimed Darwin, during the voyage of the Beagle, 'will rule as empress over the southern hemisphere'. In her capacity as tutelary empress, Australia was notably harsh in her physical and psychological treatment of her Aboriginal subjects, as well as in her representations of them. In the case of the latter, as a wide-ranging collection of studies titled *Seeing the First Australians* shows, the varieties of the Aborigines' cultural adaptions to the island continent's vast geography was denied, they were often depicted in demeaning ways, as barely human, hardly ever as noble savages in the manner of some of Ron Tamplin's writers on the South Seas, and, as in the case of the other indigenous peoples treated here, they were rapidly stereotyped.[13]

Peter Quartermaine's study of Johannes Lindt's late nineteenth century photographs of indigenous New Guinean and Australian peoples sets them within the graphic conventions of photography itself—the nature of the studio portrait, the social role of depictions of local scenes, the manner in which photographs received international exhibition, etc.—but also by reference to parallel contemporary assumptions about painting and, in turn, its role in the creation of national identities. He reminds us that photography is as subject to cultural assumptions as any other medium. Indeed, when Lindt's camera accompanied Sir Peter Scratchley's expedition to annexe New Guinea in 1885 it produced results which were at one and the same time very interesting and as confirmatory of existing prejudices as those Parke had recorded in his diary during his African expedition.

If Australia became the empress of the southern hemisphere, the western hemisphere—and ultimately almost the whole northern hemisphere—became what many commentators have referred to as the 'back yard' of the United States. And, of course, Native Americans not only lost land to the new nation but were pressed into serving the puissant Republic's ambitions in many other ways. Ironically, for instance, when President Theodore Roosevelt commissioned the sculptor Augustus Saint-Gaudens to design new coins soon after his inauguration in 1904, the figure of Liberty on the ten dollar gold piece, at his insistence, had her Phrygian cap, an iconographic necessity in French versions of Liberty, replaced by an Indian headdress. After all, claimed Roosevelt, 'American Liberty should . . . have something distinctly American about her'![14] Mick Gidley's essay explores similar paradoxes in Edward S. Curtis' photographic representation of Native Americans during the earlier part of the twentieth century. Basing much of his assessment on previously unpublished evidence, he relates the images, as they have come down to us, to both some of the contradictions in the US government's policies towards Indians and, in turn, insofar as they seem discernible, to the concerns of big American entrepreneurial interests.

There are still some writers who—usually in their faith in the mechanical aspects of the medium—insist on the unproblematically 'truthful' nature of photography. Ken Jacobson, for example, despite titling his 1989 article 'Exotic Portraits', seems not to have appreciated that the vaunted exoticism of the imagery under discussion was not inherent in the subjects of the photographs, indigenous people from a range of cultures, but was conferred upon them by the medium and its cultural context. But, for the most part, probably reciprocating the rise in sophisticated discussion of photography in general, commentators have begun to be more circumspect about photographic depictions of indigenous people.[15] Jean-Louis Comolli, in a discussion of the nature of cinematic representation, has pointed out that even more than photography, the movie, as spectacle, declares itself as a simulacrum while making the spectator work, and work hard, to maintain the belief that it is not. 'The more one knows [that one is watching a film], the more difficult it is to believe, the more it is worth it to manage to'.[16]

It is most likely that John Ford, the maker of numerous popular westerns from the 1920s to the 1960s, the subject of Richard Maltby's essay, adapted imagery from Curtis in his characteristic depictions of Native Americans. He certainly borrowed from Frederic Remington and other painters who worked at least almost directly, as we misleadingly say, from life.[17] But it is clearer in Ford's case that his work treated the Past—was more overtly a re-presentation. Hence Richard Maltby's emphasis on the relationship between Ford's movies and, on the one hand, history and, on the other, myth. He shows that, in depictions of the West in general, these categories have not been as differentiated as we might think. While rightly underlining the specifically cinematic aspects of Ford's achievement, the particular forms of spectacle on offer and the audience response made possible, and allowing for other features possibly unique to him, the essay shows that, in a variety of important ways, Ford's westerns plugged not only into a set of Hollywood movie conventions which might be partly accounted for by genre theory but also into an ongoing system of representation of Indians that manifested itself in a variety of media, from romances by James Fenimore Cooper to dime novels, but which changed according to the specific historical context. It is important to note that while Ford was exceptional, he was also typical. Maltby certainly demonstrates that Ford's way of representing indigenous people cannot be separated from significant tensions in American society, especially concerning race, ethnic identity and sexuality.

After reading these introductory indications of the contents of this book, the reader might well be excused for wondering whether it is ever possible for a member of one culture, perhaps especially a member of a dominant culture, to represent another culture—or, even, just to hear the voices and truly see the sights of another culture. 'If the ways of seeing in different communities are in conflict because their interpretive practices reflect incommensurable presuppositions about the human situation, can such communities understand each other?' asks Paul B. Armstrong. 'Can one culture use its own terms to say something about another culture without engaging in a hostile act of appropriation or without simply reflecting itself and not engaging the otherness of the Other? . . . But . . . can we ever escape our provincial islands and navigate between worlds?' I would submit that the first step, as exemplified by the essays themselves in this collection, must be to become aware— and ever more aware—of the problematics of the representational act itself.[18]

The second, at least for members of habitually colonialist groups, might be to attend to the voices of those 'others' as they express what the Nigerian novelist Chinua Achebe has termed 'The Song of Ourselves'. Of the sight of Africans seen in the awesome forest along the river bank, Conrad's narrator in *Heart of Darkness* had this to say: 'It was unearthly, and the men were—No, they were not inhuman. Well, you know, that was the worst of it—this suspicion of them not being inhuman'. Achebe, understandably reacting adversely to such hedged acknowledgements of the full humanity of fellow Africans, has discerned not just a desire, but a *need* for African writers to celebrate the continued presence of African peoples in the continent. Cultural historians like Ana Maria Alonso have shown at the theoretical level, if with graphic personal testimony, that a people's social memory is integral to the creation of their social meaning, that their own representations of the past are central to the very constitution of social groups and to the maintenance of social, as well as individual, identities. At the aesthetic level, so to speak, this is the formidable task undertaken by Achebe and other indigenous artists. Ngugi wa Thiong'o—who, interestingly, has also recorded the disquiet Conrad caused him, despite his admiration for the older novelist's narrative virtuosity—advocates the further step of 'writing' in indigenous languages in a manner as sensitive as possible to the oral properties of both language and culture.[19]

In many respects, such strategies demand much from the person from another culture who wishes to learn something of the original culture— various translations, from oral to written, from one language to another, from the conventions of one medium, with all its local nuances, to another, and so on, each attended by literally incommunicable losses. And this does not, of course, completely answer Armstrong's rightly anguished question; the means of transmission, for example, even for Ngugi, cannot be a wholly indigenous form, and Armstrong and others have stressed the necessity for acceptance—indeed, the desirability—of a 'to-and-fro' movement, a 'play' between and across forms of cultural expression. It is such play or intertextuality which produces what that 'hybridity' of structure and meaning which the authors of *The Empire Writes Back* call 'the primary characteristic of all post-colonial texts, whatever their source'. Cognate procedures are apparent in other, non-literary, arts; for instance, Ruth Phillips has described the interplay practiced by Native American women beadworkers in Victorian Canada between the decorative associations of flowers for their white patrons and the symbolic suggestiveness of such natural forms in the indigenous culture. Anyone who listens to contemporary popular music, such as reggae, salsa, or countless other forms, will have to acknowledge a similar 'hybridity'.[20]

Octavio Paz, the Mexican writer, has both 'written back' against the hegemony of North American culture and repeatedly reflected upon both the local meaning of being Mexican and the trans-cultural issues raised here. In 'The Other Mexico' (1970) he writes: 'Mexican-ness is no more than another example, another variety, of that changing, identical, single, plural creature that each is, all are, none is. Man/ men: perpetual oscillation. The diversity of characters, temperaments, histories, civilisations makes of man, men.' And when he continues this peroration there is an invocation of the idea of the mask, somewhat reminiscent of the Siqueiros painting, and a concern with pronouns not unrelated to that which we have already encountered in Said and those in his wake: 'we are like this, they are like that, etc.' Despite Paz' plethora of pronouns in what follows, it will be irritating to many that they fail, even then, to embrace both genders—but this in turn illustrates the very difficulties he is discussing and we are considering. Language too, of course, is a medium of representation, as shot through with cultural assumptions as any other, and, as a small lesson on the tyranny of pronouns, the reader might consider the varying practices in this respect adopted by the contributors to the present book.

'And the plural is resolved, is dissolved, in the singular: I, you, he, vanishing as soon as pronounced', Paz writes. 'Pronouns, like nouns, are masks, and there is no one behind them—except, perhaps, an instantaneous we which is a twinkling of an equally fleeting it. But while we live we can escape neither masks nor nouns and pronouns: we are inseparable from our fictions, our features. We are condemned to invent a mask and to discover afterward that the mask is our true visage.'[21] Paz' words here may appear initially enigmatic—even persistently enigmatic—as well as profound. But for someone envisaging the difficulties and rewards of a continuing investigation of the varieties of human cultures, they may also thereby serve as a point of contemplation—an appropriate enticement rather than a mere conclusion.

NOTES

1. E.S. Curtis to E.S. Meany, November 19, 1911, Meany Papers, University of Washington Libraries, Seattle. A study of Curtis' performance may be found in Mick Gidley, 'The Vanishing Race in Sight and Sound: Edward S. Curtis's Musicale of North American Indian Life', in Jack Salzman, ed., *Prospects*, Vol. 12 (Cambridge and New York, 1987), pp. 59-87.

2. See Hanna Fenichel Pitkin, *The Concept of Representation* (Berkeley, Los Angeles, London, 1967), especially pp. 63-115; Howard S. Becker, 'Telling about Society', in his *Doing Things Together* (Evanston, IL, 1986), pp. 121-35; and W.J.T. Mitchell, 'Representation', in Frank Lentricchia and Thomas McLaughlin, eds., *Critical Terms for Literary Study* (Chicago and London, 1990), pp. 11-22.

3. See, for example, David Freedberg, *The Power of Images: Studies in the History and Theory of Response* (Chicago and London, 1989), especially the final chapter.

4. In this significant sense, the distinction drawn above between an entity called reality and a domain called representation should not be maintained with absolute rigidity; perhaps a term such as 'discursive practice', with its attendant conflation of cause and effect, might be more appropriate; see Paul A. Bové, 'Discourse', in Lentricchia and McLaughlin, pp. 50-65, an essay which introduces related issues beyond the scope of the present book.

5. Mitchell, 'Representation', p. 15; also, Pitkin, cited above, deals primarily with political representation.

6. Edward W. Said, *Orientalism* (New York, 1978). For consideration of the effects of Said's work, see Francis Barker *et al*, *Europe and its Others*, Papers from a Conference at the University of Essex, 2 volumes (Colchester, 1985). James Clifford, 'On *Orientalism*' in his *The Predicament of Culture: Twentieth Century Ethnography, Literature and Art* (Cambridge, MA and London, 1988), p. 258.

7. See, for example, Talal Asad, ed., *Anthropology and the Colonial Encounter* (London, 1973); several others are cited in Clifford, 'On *Orientalism*', p. 256. See also Edward W. Said, 'Representing the Colonized: Anthropology's Interlocutors', *Critical Inquiry*, 15 (Winter 1989), 205-25.

8. See, for example, James Clifford and George E. Marcus, eds., *Writing Culture: The Poetics and Politics of Ethnography* (Berkeley, Los Angeles, London, 1986) and Clifford Geertz, *Works and Lives: The Anthropologist as Author* (Stanford, CA, 1988). Johannes Fabian, *Time and the Other: How Anthropology Makes its Object* (New York, 1983).

9. Becker, p. 126 and *passim*.

10. See H.N. Fairchild, *The Noble Savage: A Study in Romantic Naturalism* (New York, 1928) and numerous subsequent discussions, including David Murray, *Forked Tongues: Speech, Writing and Representation in North American Indian Texts* (London and Bloomington, 1991), p. 35-7.

11. See, for example, Alan Sandison, *The Wheel of Empire: A Study of the*

Imperial Idea in Some Late Nineteenth Century and Early Twentieth Century Fiction (London, 1967); Martin Green, *Dreams of Adventure, Deeds of Empire* (London, 1980); and Hugh Ridley, *Images of Imperial Rule* (London and New York, 1983). A notable exception is James Clifford's 'On Ethnographic Self-Fashioning: Conrad and Malinowski', in *The Predicament of Culture*, pp. 52-113.

12. Twain to Charles L. Webster, November 11, 1885, Mark Twain Papers, Bancroft Library (Berkeley, CA.). The book in question was published, with Daggett credited as author, as *King Kalahaua's Hawaiian Legends* (1886). Bernard Smith, *European Vision and the South Pacific 1768-1850* (Oxford, 1960).

13. Charles Darwin, *Journal of Researches into the Natural History and Geology of the Countries Visited during the Voyage of H.M.S. 'Beagle' Round the World* (London, 1890), p. 368. Ian Donaldson and Tamsin Donaldson, eds., *Seeing the First Australians* (Sydney, London and Boston, 1985).

14. See Willard B. Gatewood, 'Theodore Roosevelt and the Coinage Controversy', *American Quarterly*, 18 (Spring 1966), p. 37.

15. Ken Jacobson, 'Exotic Portraits', *The Photohistorian* (1989), pp. 48-52. The general works invoked here would include, for example, Susan Sontag, *On Photography* (New York and London, 1977) and Philip Stokes, 'A Quiet Message, Strangely Told: The Photograph as Communication', *exposure* vol 25, No. 4 (Winter 1987), pp. 16-24. Worthwhile shorter treatments of ethnographic photographs include David Green, 'Classified Subjects', *Ten.8*, 14 (1984), pp. 30-7; Jill Lloyd, 'Old Photographs, Vanished Peoples and Stolen Potatoes', *Art Monthly*, 83 (February 1985), pp. 13-6; Mick Gidley, 'North American Indian Photographs/Images', *American Indian Culture and Research Journal*, 9, no3 (1985), pp. 37-47; and items in volume 3, number 2 (1990) of *Visual Anthropology*, a special issue edited by Joanna Cohan Scherer.

16. Jean-Louis Comolli, 'Machines of the Visible', in Teresa de Lauretis and Stephen Heath, eds. *The Cinematic Apparatus* (London, 1980), pp. 121-42.

17. See Edward Buscombe, 'Painting the Legend: Frederic Remington and the Western', *Cinema Journal*, 23 (Summer 1984), pp. 12-27; and William Howze, 'John Ford's Celluloid Canvas', *Southwest Media Review*, (Spring 1985), pp. 20-5.

18. Paul B. Armstrong, 'Play and Cultural Differences', *Kenyon Review* NS 13 (Winter 1991), p. 157. An example of good practice in this respect is David Murray, *Forked Tongues*, cited above.

19. Joseph Conrad, *Heart of Darkness* (Harmondsworth, 1980), p. 69. Chinua Achebe, 'The Song of Ourselves', *New Statesman & Society*, February 9, 1990, pp. 30-2. Ana Maria Alonso, 'The Effects of Truth: Re-Presentations of the Past and the Imagining of Community', *Journal of Historical Sociology*, 1 (March 1988), pp. 33-57. Ngugi wa Thiong'o, *Decolonising the Mind: The Politics of Language in African Literature* (London, 1986), especially pp. 63-86.

20. See Armstrong, 'Play', pp. 159-71, for a subtle argument which is both an extension and a critique of Said's position. A key passage of *The Empire Writes Back: Theory and Practice in Post-Colonial Literature* (1989) by Bill Ashcroft, Gareth Griffiths, and Helen Tiffin is excerpted in Dennis Walder, ed., *Literature in the Modern World: Critical Essays and Documents* (Oxford and New York, 1990), pp. 298-303. Ruth Phillips, unpublished paper delivered at the European Association for American Studies conference, London, April 1990.

21. Octavio Paz, 'The Other Mexico', trans. Lysander Kemp, in *The Labyrinth of Solitude* (Harmondsworth, 1990), p. 216.

STEPHANIE SMILES

A Native American in Stone: The Simcoe Memorial in Exeter Cathedral

The South Quire Aisle in Exeter Cathedral contains a striking memorial to the first Lieutenant Governor of Upper Canada, Colonel John Graves Simcoe (1752–1806). Erected by subscription, it is a signed work by the sculptor, John Flaxman (1755–1826), who probably came to Exeter in 1815 to supervise its completion.[1] The memorial consists of an area of entablature topped with an arrangement of crossed flags and the Simcoe family arms. A panel within the area of entablature includes a simply-elucidated decorative pattern of a four-petalled flower repeated across its surface and intersected by diagonal lines forming a diamond-shaped lattice around each flower. The effect is that of a brocaded surface which harmonises and complements the other elements in the sculpture. In the centre of the panel is a small portrait bust in bas-relief of Governor Simcoe. A gothic canopy with appropriate tracery surmounts the central panel and the tracery extends to the niches at the sides. Unique and eye-catching, the design by Flaxman is distinctive in one other particular aspect. In the right hand niche stands the figure of a Native American man dressed in simple attire and carrying a small tomahawk in his right hand (*illus. 1*). As far as I have been able to discover, Flaxman's employment of a Native American figure in the Simcoe Memorial represents only the third instance during the period 1750 to 1815 where Native American figures were depicted in monumental sculpture in England.[2]

The relative absence of the Native American figure in this area of the fine arts points to issues of Native American representation in general. That is, in spite of the crucial role played by the Native American in helping to bring about successful military campaigns, trading ventures and settlement strategies in America, his importance as a historical figure was not reflected in an area such as monumental sculpture. It is significant that in some way his person was not felt to be a suitable subject for interpretation in stone and marble in England at this time. Specifically, the proliferation of more decorative and ephemeral items which displayed his features helped to create a standard visual type symbolic of all Native Americans. This standard type, a semi-nude figure given a feather skirt and crown, would influence many forms of representation of the Native American, including those of the 'higher' forms of artistic practice. To the extent that a relative absence of representation in the more serious art forms, such as painting and sculpture, and a proliferation of images in the more frivolous decorative art forms constitutes a marginalisation of the Native American figure in art, it reflects the negligence of British policy-making with regard to the treatment of Native Americans and the realities of their existence.

In reviewing the whole corpus of Native American imagery in this period it is evident that in the vast majority of cases Native American figures are only given expression in order to provide appropriate exotic colour or to titillate a jaded sensibility. Actual Native American people and their needs were not adequately recognised in the policies of British colonial administration and this 'marginal' status finds an apt echo in their artistic representation. With a limited number of precedents to the work and an even greater process of marginalisation of the Native American figure tending both to contain and regulate its appearance in sculpture, it is all the more poignant that Flaxman should have chosen to give elucidation to a Native American personage in one of his sculptures. The design and execution of the Simcoe Memorial represents a break with tradition, an unwillingness to accept outmoded formulae and a reworking of plastic relationships handed down from the antique.

Of the other two existing works made during this period, it is Robert Adam's Townshend Monument (1761) in Westminster Abbey that most concerns us here (*illus. 2*). Lieutenant Roger Townshend had perished in the battle for Ticonderoga in 1759. Like General James Wolfe, who was killed in the same year, Townshend exemplified the terrific loss in terms of human life that had been sustained in order to gain dominance on the North American continent. The eventual successes of various military campaigns in America came to be associated with a growing feeling of Empire in Britain as she spread her influence to many parts of the world. The Native American figures who appear in the Townshend Monument are in keeping with this feeling of influence abroad, for they are posed in the attitude of classical support figures whose role it is to carry the casket of the deceased military personage. In this way, the Townshend 'Indians' are linked to the Roman practice of including figures of captives or conquered slaves in the design of sculptural edifices and monuments. The placement of Native American figures in a design which likens them to classical caryatids can only be detrimental to the perception of them as beings separate from a European tradition. Native Americans were not alone in being adopted for this purpose. In the late seventeenth-century, a monument erected to the memory of the Grand Master of the Knights of St. John, Nicolas Cotoner, in St. John's Co-Cathedral in Malta, shows the images of a Black African and Turkish slave crouching in chains under the weight of the plinth.[3] The iconographic significance of this arrangement would not have been lost on its viewers. Adams' inclusion of the two Native American males, reminiscent of the Della Valle Satyrs, would have triggered in its viewers' minds an association with the Imperial pretensions of the classical past and would have reminded onlookers that Native Americans had taken part in the wars as allies of both the British and the French. It is a less than sympathetic portrayal of Native American features, in spite of Adam's attention to ethnographic detail, and aligns them with all foreign peoples who at one time or another had become subjugated to Imperial rule.[4]

In spite of the success and artistic influence of Adam's Townshend figures, Flaxman's design for the Simcoe Memorial tapped new and previously unexplored areas of representation. Although the Townshend Monument is the one work containing Native American figures Flaxman knew and admired, he chose not to follow it.[5] While the figures in the Abbey monument symbolic of the Native American involvment in the Canadian wars may have been influential in Flaxman's decision to include such a figure in his own work, the results of his efforts still reveal a tremendous break with tradition. The Canadian Indian in the Simcoe Memorial assumes a completely different role with respect to the European figures in the composition; he is given traits that only the noblest of Europeans are allowed to bear and he speaks with clear issue of the important role played by Native Americans in the colonial affairs of that era.

In the fifty years between the Townshend commission and the work for the Simcoe Memorial, important changes occurred in the relationship the British held with the Native American groups which made possible Flaxman's new interpretation. During the Revolutionary Wars, 1775–1783, many Eastern Woodland tribes became involved in the conflict. Some groups literally disintegrated as they were torn between joining one side or the other. However, when the fighting stopped, Native American representatives were left out of the peace negotiations. In the Paris conference of 1783 Native claims to the lands west of the Appalachians were ignored and the 'American negotiators . . . asserted their sovereignty over the lands of the interior.'[6] The British had made many promises to their allies during the war in order to gain their support for planned military campaigns and it was all too evident to critics of British colonial rule that the Europeans had abandoned their sworn allies. Guilt at what had taken place immediately after the cessation of the conflict caused certain members of the British colonial government to make appeals on behalf of the Indian groups by attempting to find a place for their settlement within the provinces of Canada. Simcoe was one of these colonial officials who felt that the Native Americans, particularly staunch British allies such as the Mohawk, should be resettled. As late as the 1790's, General Frederick Haldimand, Governor of Quebec, delayed the transition of frontier forts from British to American control and thereby helped to cushion Native American claims.

There is also evidence that the administration in England was sympathetic. The Prime Minister, Lord North, wrote, 'These People are justly entitled to our Peculiar attention and it would be far from either generous or just in us, after our cession of their Territories and Hunting grounds, to forsake them.'[7] The sympathetic strain in the thought of the time would grow as the problems generated by contact with the indigenous peoples were less and less a truly British concern. In other words, now that the British government and the Crown no longer had complete jurisdiction over the tribes living within the boundaries of the United States, it became easier to recognise admirable qualities possessed by the Native American peoples, a recognition made more readily as part of the burgeoning cult of the Primitive that was so influential in the late eighteenth-century. In addition to this growing recognition of the virtues of the Native American way of life, there was the more important realisation that this life was under threat of extinction. It is within this changed climate and atmosphere of acceptance that Flaxman's work and choice of subject-matter for the Simcoe commission must be viewed.

Flaxman's memorial is to a colonial administrator and military leader who entered office at a crucial point in the development of Canada's relations with the indigenous peoples of the Canadian border regions. Flaxman thus shows an obvious interest in depicting Native Americans as a testament to Governor Simcoe's policies. The artist had had experience in the depiction of foreign or 'exotic' peoples before the Simcoe work, especially in his commission from the Raja Sarfogi for a full-length, lifesize portrait (1803–5) and in his monuments to Sir William Jones (1796) and the Reverend Christian Frederick Schwartz

(1805). David Irwin has pointed to the care which Flaxman took over the Jones monument in making several life studies of Hindu men in order to achieve ethnographic authenticity. Preliminary drawings also exist for the Simcoe Memorial which indicate similarly that the sculptor had some first-hand experience of Native American dress and ornamentation.[8] One of the two drawings for the Simcoe Memorial is in a finished state and can serve as evidence of Flaxman's thoughts concerning the design of his piece (*illus. 3*). In the drawing the artist has given the Native American figure accoutrements that would align him with many of the Eastern Woodland groups. Of all these groups, it seems likely that Flaxman would have hoped to approximate Iroquois dress in his work. The figure's specific traits in the drawing are the ornaments worn on the head and neck, the belted tunic (or shirt and breech-cloth) worn on the body and the tomahawk in his left hand. Ornamentation about the head and face consists of a coxcomb or feather head-dress attached somewhere near the back of the head and a long piece of shell or other rigid ornament attached at the ear in an unascertainable fashion. The belt around the waist of the figure appears to be decorated with a repeated design of a geometric pattern and again this may be an approximation of a true Native American pattern. Other marks of attribution are the beaded necklace worn around the neck and the gorget attached to it.

The Native American figure in Flaxman's drawing is also in keeping with images of Eastern Woodland tribal personages who came to England previous to 1815. It seems likely that the artist would have been familiar with some of these images as there were several commissioned portraits of certain visitors and many prints taken after these. During the visit of Lieutenant Henry Timberlake and a group of Cherokee representatives in 1762 several artists made portraits of some of the individual Native American leaders and the graphic representations of these Cherokee 'Chiefs' were extremely numerous.[9] In these works, there is a certain regularity of presentation where the figures appear in clothes that combine Native American and European elements (*illus. 4*). It is significant for the original drawings for the Simcoe Memorial that the image of a fully clothed and distinguished Native American male was current at this time. Also, in several cases in the portraits of the Cherokees their hair is plucked over the top of the head, ornaments are attached to their heads and ears and they wear the sign of attachment to the British cause, a metal gorget with the arms of George III. Flaxman's initial design for the Native American figure follows this pattern in that the pose of the figure, one arm covered in a blanket or cape, is the same as that of the earlier portraits. Similarly, the artist gives his figure a combination of Native and European made clothes, he makes reference to the symbol of alliance with the British in the gorget worn at the neck, and the figure sports head and neck ornamentation in keeping with what was known of Eastern Woodland dress in this era.

On the other hand, there is the possibility that the sculptor worked from his memory of an individual Native American leader as there is some chance he would have met a Mohawk Indian in the course of his life, namely, Joseph Brant or Thayendangegea. Brant had created a sensation in that he was accepted into fashionable circles, joined the Freemasons and had his portrait painted by several important artists.[10] He was a friend of the influential Sir William Johnson, Superintendent of Indian Affairs in the Northern Colonies (1756–1774), and supported the British during the Revolutionary Wars. He visited England twice, first in 1775–6 and again in 1786. The reception given Brant during his diplomatic mission of 1776, in the company of Colonel Guy Johnson, had practical consequences in that Mohawk support was needed for success of the British campaigns. Thus colonial leaders were eager to give this influential personage the respect and deference he was due. At the end of the Wars, Brant was allowed to settle on his own land along the Grand River in Canada, the reward given him for his services. Brant must have exuded a penetrating charm.[11]

Brant's portrait by the artist George Romney (dated 1775–6) shows the Native American man standing erect regaled in ceremonial accoutrement with feathers fashioned in his headband, a silver gorget worn about his neck and a tomahawk held at his side (*illus. 5*). Portraying with great skill Brant's intensity of expression and unswerving gaze, the portrait has the power to captivate and enchant viewers while at the same time reminding them of the military importance of his presence. As Flaxman met Romney sometime in 1775, and remained close to him, he may have met Brant personally and witnessed the portrait. The Indian figure in Flaxman's sketch for the Simcoe piece has some points in common with the Romney portrait of Joseph Brant. Both are wearing a draped cloth or cape over one shoulder, each assumes a dignified pose, a gorget hangs at the neck of both figures and a feather head-dress of some kind adorns both. Furthermore, the Indian in Flaxman's drawing looks as though he is wearing a European-made shirt under his tunic and a similar shirt is worn by Brant in several of the portraits. Although the Simcoe work was done nearly forty years after the portrait by Romney, Flaxman could still have looked to the engraved portrait of Brant for accuracy of detail and for inspiration.[12]

Finally, it was Governor Simcoe's relationship to the Native American groups under his jurisdiction, which included the Mohawk settlement on the Grand River in Ontario, that may have induced Flaxman to make a visual reference to the historical character of Brant. As leader of the Queen's Rangers (1777), Simcoe probably commanded Native American auxiliaries at some time in his military career. Unfortunately, he assumed the office of Lieutenant Governor at the very time when relations with Native Americans were at their most distant (1791). Many Indian groups had taken up the issues of land rights in the era after 1783 and this had resulted in the post-war hostilities of the 1790's; hence Simcoe's moves to provide land for those peoples who had remained loyal to the British cause. Brant was introduced to Simcoe by the Duke of Northumberland and Simcoe would later assess the motives of the Native American leader in this way: 'He considers the Indian Interests as the first Object—that as a second, tho' very inferior one, He prefers the British, in a certain degree, to the people of the U.S.'[13] During the time the monument to Simcoe was being commissioned, the Native American presence on the North American continent re-entered public consciousness. The war with the United States during 1812 again saw the involvement of Native American groups in the fighting along the Canadian border. Some of the same groups who had supported the British in the 1770's again fought alongside British troops in battles up and down the continent. Flaxman would have been aware of the role they played in campaigns in Canada and therefore would have seen their relevance for a sculptural work of this kind.

However, in spite of the inclusion of the Native American's weapon, his tomahawk, and his stern gaze and countenance, the Native American figure in Flaxman's work has a non-aggressive appearance (*illus. 6*). This comes about largely because of the context in which the figure has been elucidated. In the iconography of tomb sculpture, the niches flanking the tomb traditionally held the images of saints or the high-ranking clergy which sanctity and religious custom had demanded. In Flaxman's monument the figures in the niches act more as witnesses to the Governor's achievements, giving testimony to his policies of appeasement and humanitarian ideals. Their calm and dignified pose is in keeping with this function and as a result, the Native American figure achieves a monumental *gravitas* quite different from the figures in the Townshend Monument. Indeed, the two figures on each side of the central portrait bust of Simcoe almost assume a greater importance than the Governor himself as they are much larger and nearly carved in the round.

A Native American in Stone

The most notable difference in the Flaxman design after its transformation to marble is the toning down and deletion of certain ethnographic details on the Indian figure. The head and neck ornamentation has been relinquished in order to present the more smooth appearance of a bare head and shoulders. The braids which are retained at the back of the head are only noticeable when close to the memorial and when viewed from the side. Technical concerns may have prompted the deletion of the feather head-dress but this cannot be the entire reason for elimination of detail. The artist appears to have been in quest of a more profound impact by use of a clear, uncluttered line. What was lost in the reduction of the Native American traits—and thus the 'exotic' quality of the work—was gained in the impact of the sculpture as a whole. Flaxman's use of the intervening space between figures and the background gives harmony to the work. The Native American occupies an important role in that he balances the composition and invites comparison with his compatriot in the opposite niche. More important though, he is given an equal position within the framework of the piece and is not allowed to assume an inferior role with respect to the other figures as one of support or colourful relief. He stands alongside the other figure in companionship and mutual respect just as he had done in life when he fought beside the British in their wars.

Further elements which counteract a traditional reading of the Native American figure are the drapery given him and his facial expression. The drapery works within the piece to enhance a feeling of stability and gives the figure a noble bearing. Sculptural use of drapery in the form of togas, chitons, robes or cloaks has associative qualities that connect the subject who wears them with the antique past and allies them with a tradition of representation originally thought appropriate only for nobility or high ranking officials. Flaxman's use of a draped blanket as the only adornment on his Native American figure connects his work with the antique and gives the blanket a toga-like appearance. Indeed, the connotative power which such drapery exerts over the viewer and its influence on the sculpture as a whole almost overwhelms the other figures and elements in the design. It creates a concentration of effect within the Native American figure, whose rather mature features give him a distinguished air in contrast to the more youthful appearance of the infantryman. Finally, the expression on the face of the warrior, appearing calm and somewhat thoughtful, further removes any sense of harm that the tomahawk or his 'Indian-ness' could incite. Contrasted with the more sullen expressions on the faces of the Townshend figures, this portrait of a Native American is sympathetic and idealised.

In designing the Townshend figures, working from the studies he had made from a captured Native American boy, Adam had shown sensitivity to Native American adornment, but he still had not let the figures he employed exceed the bounds of their known role in art.[14] Flaxman, despite the images of Indians which existed all around him via the decorative arts, in the furnishings, tableware and ornamentation in the households of his friends and patrons, had another vision which became translated in his work on the Simcoe Memorial into a statement about the equality of Native American peoples and the need to recognise their roles in colonial affairs on the North American continent.

NOTES

1. Flaxman's account book, now in Columbia University Library, states that total payment for the work amounted to £950, £320 of which he received as a first payment on May 27, 1811. For the full account-book entry see John Physick, *Designs for English Sculpture 1680—1860* (London, 1969), p.175. See *Trewman's Exeter Flying Post*, November 29, 1815, postscript. Local papers noted the completion of the Memorial to General Simcoe and one mentioned that the work was 'executed' by Flaxman, thereby leading this researcher to conclude that the artist travelled to Exeter to direct the monument's completion.

2. This author has found the nomenclature commonly employed when referring to the indigenous peoples of America somewhat problematic. While the term 'Native American' is perhaps somewhat more descriptive than the term 'American Indian', both elicit problems of definition and racial stereotype. The former term has been used in this article when a reference to the abstract notion of an 'original' inhabitant of the Americas was necessary; the word 'Indian' has been used when contemporary accounts have done so. Other than the Townshend Monument in Westminster Abbey, there exists only one other example of the sculptural use of Native American figures in England of this period: that of the monument to Cornet Geary in Great Bookham, Surrey, which was erected in 1776. The figures appear in relief on the base and the work is unsigned.

3. Hugh Honour, *The New Golden Land: European Images of America from the Discoveries to the Present Time* (New York, 1975), p.129. See J. Bartolo, *The Co-Cathedral of St. John*, 4th ed. (Valletta, 1980), pp.33-4, which includes an illustration.

4. See Francis Haskell and Nicholas Penny, *Taste and the Antique: The Lure of Classical Sculpture, 1500-1900* (New Haven and London, 1981), pp.302-3, which includes an illustration; the figures of the Satyrs act as a pair and are posed with one arm raised above their heads to grasp the overhead support. Honour, *The New Golden Land*, pp.128-9, suggests that Adam probably

based his final design on studies made of a live figure, the Native American boy brought back to England by Townshend's brother, George Townshend.

5. The influence of Adam's design on the accoutrements given other Native American figures can be seen in illustrations such as those included in Jonathan Carver's *Travels Through the Interior Parts of North America, in the Years, 1766, 1767, and 1768* (London: Printed for the Author, 1778). J.T. Smith, *Nollekens and His Times*, Vol. II (London, 1828), p.308, quotes an anecdote that 'Flaxman used to say he would give something for the possession of the name of the artist who executed the sculptural parts of this monument which he considered to be one of the finest productions of art in the Abbey.'

6. See Colin G. Calloway, *Crown and Calumet: British—Indian Relations, 1783–1815* (Norman and London, 1987), p.6. Quotation from Robert M. Utley and Wilcomb E. Washburn, *The History of the Indian Wars* (London, 1977), p.120.

7. *John Graves Simcoe 1752-1806* (Guidebook to the Wolford Memorial Chapel, Devonshire, England) (Toronto, n.d.), p.5. Quotation from Utley and Washburn, *History*, p.121.

8. Two drawings, one a slight sketch, are held in the Victoria and Albert Museum's Prints and Drawings collection. The drawing discussed here is no. 8967A, 10½" × 13⅛", and is in pen and ink and wash. Flaxman must also have made models for the two standing figures, perhaps in terracotta, and to have been pleased with the work, for he exhibited figures of a 'Canadian Indian' and a 'British Volunteer' in the 1814 exhibition at the Royal Academy. See Algernon Graves, *The Royal Academy of Arts: A Complete Dictionary of Contributors and Their Work from its Foundation in 1769 to 1904*, Vol.III (London, 1905), p.124. For the Jones commission see David Irwin, *John Flaxman 1755-1826* (London, 1979), ps.122 and 142.

9. Joshua Reynolds' diary for June 1762 records as one of his sitters 'The King of the Cherokees'. This must correspond with the painting by Reynolds now in the Thomas Gilcrease Museum in Tulsa, Oklahoma, of a figure known as 'Scyacust Ukah'. For Reynolds' diary entry see Algernon Graves and William Vine Cronin, *A History of the Works of Sir Joshua Reynolds, P.R.A.*, Vol.IV (London, 1899-1901), p.1533. Another painting in the Gilcrease Museum is of 'Cunne Shote' by Francis Parsons. This personage is another member of the Cherokee delegation which visited England in 1762. A mezzotint engraving was made by James MacArdell after the portrait by Parsons. Other engravings exist which purport to portray the 'King' or Outacity (Ostenaco).

10. J.R. Fawcett Thompson, 'Thayendanegea the Mohawk and his Several Portraits,' *Connoisseur*, 170 (1969), pp.49-53.

11. Carolyn Thomas Foreman, *Indians Abroad, 1493—1938* (Norman, 1943), pp.94-6. Colonel Guy Johnson was the nephew and son-in-law of Sir William Johnson and was acting Superintendent of Indian Affairs in 1776 after the death of his uncle in 1774. Thompson, *Connoisseur*, describes at

least six separate paintings made of Brant. It is also known that Francis Rigaud exhibited a portrait of Joseph Brant in the Royal Academy in 1786 but this work has not been traced.

12. Irwin, *John Flaxman*, p.6. A mezzotint by J.R. Smith after Romney's portrait of Joseph Brant was published in February, 1779.

13. Of Simcoe's introduction to Brant see Carl F. Klinck and James J. Talman, eds., *The Journal of Major John Norton* (Toronto, 1970), p.lxxxiii. Simcoe's assessment of Brant comes from Calloway, *Crown and Calumet*, p.239.

14. See note 4.

TIM YOUNGS

The Medical Officer's Diary: Travel and Travail with the Self in Africa

In the introduction to a recent collection of essays, *Imperial Medicine and Indigenous Societies*, David Arnold has claimed that: 'In the closing years of the nineteenth century medicine became a demonstration of the superior political, technical and military power of the West, and hence a celebration of imperialism itself'.[1] Since the powers and ideologies of imperialism are often reflected in the writings of contemporary travellers and explorers, I want in this essay to test Arnold's statement against an example of a literary form which may be seen to perform a diagnostic, if not therapeutic, function: the diary. The case I shall focus on is that of Thomas Heazle Parke, medical officer to Henry Morton Stanley's Emin Pasha Relief Expedition, whose journal was published in 1891.[2]

This expedition lasted from the beginning of 1887 to the end of 1889. Its ostensible motive was the rescue of Emin Pasha, who in 1878 had been appointed Governor of Equatoria, the southernmost province of Sudan, by General Gordon. The latter's fatal defeat at the hands of the Madhist forces in 1885 and the subsequent evacuation of the Sudan helped create the conditions for the projection of an image of Emin as an isolated man abandoned by the Egyptian Government, and whose relief would atone for the humiliating failure of the British to save Gordon.

More than twenty thousand pounds was raised for the support of the expedition, around half of it coming from the Egyptian Government, and much of the remainder from the Emin Pasha Relief Committee, the driving force behind which was William Mackinnon, the founder of the British India Steam Navigation Company and later President of the British East Africa Company, the interests and membership of which overlapped closely with those of the Relief Committee. Underlying the proclaimed reasons for the expedition was the hope of commercial gain from the large stock of ivory believed to be held by Emin, and from a series of land treaties which were to be carried out with African chiefs. Stanley was also acting for King Leopold of Belgium, exploring the possibilities of annexing Equatoria to the Congo.

The route decided upon by Stanley was to follow the Congo up to its confluence with the Aruwimi River, then up the Aruwimi to the Yambuya, where the Rear Column was left, through the daunting Ituri forest to Lake Albert and up the lake towards Emin's headquarters at Wadelai. But there resulted a mixture of deep farce and tragedy. Emin, once met with, vacillated embarrassingly and had to be persuaded to be relieved. At a banquet in the port of Bagamoyo to celebrate the accomplishment of the mission, the short-sighted Pasha fell twenty feet from a window, nearly killing himself. Only two hundred and ninety refugees from the Equatorial Province reached Bagamoyo out of five hundred and seventy who had been in the expedition's care at Kavalli. Two of Stanley's ten white subordinates, James Jameson and Edmund Barttelot, did not survive the expedition and half of the seven hundred Africans failed to return from it, leading to widespread outrage and severe criticism of Stanley's conduct and judgement, especially regarding the Rear Column, which was stranded for several months with no word from Stanley and little aid from Tippu-Tib, the ivory and slave dealer whose support Stanley had enlisted for them. Through starvation, food poisoning and disease, the Rear Column lost more than one hundred and fifty men, sixty per cent of its number. Bitter disputes arose between the families of the two dead white officers and Stanley, and the controversy widened into a fierce debate about Britain's aims and methods in Africa, the military and commercial character of the expedition being particularly condemned. Nevertheless, from a European point of view, the expedition helped map areas of Central Africa and 'discovered' the snow-capped Ruwenzori, the so-called 'Mountains of the Moon'. And the sufferings in the Great Central African Forest provided a powerful image of redemption and of man's capacity to survive, if not subdue, a hostile environment.

It has been said of nineteenth-century writing on Africa that it was a 'discovery on paper', a phenomenon which, one might argue, is matched by the role performed by the diary for the self.[3] Both assertions are true of Parke's journal, which also presents the literary construction and social affirmation of an individual and cultural identity. The chronological record of the events of the journey shares its pattern with biography, whilst the centredness of the self in a foreign land imposing upon a succession of environments and their inhabitants reinforces cultural and physical imperialism.[4] This point is made even more apparent on the few occasions when, through illness, Parke is briefly unable to write (pp.44, 255, 288, 439), since these short gaps are later recorded and made part of the narrative. Such silences may, then, be followed by the re-emergence of the self through the exercise of observation and analysis. Thus the entry for 24 October 1888:

> I have not been able to write anything for the last couple of days, I have been so weakened by my fever. It comes on every day, about eleven or twelve o'clock (noon), with a temperature of 103°F., which continues till about 1 P.M., when it falls to the normal level. There seems to be no ending to this fever; quinine has, apparently, no antidotal power; and I am fairly burnt up by the combustion that is going on within me. The result is that I am as pale as a sheet, from haematuria; giddy, from anaemia and debility; and unable to walk more than a hundred yards without resting. It is now the sixteenth day of this fever. (p.286)

And when he tells us in retrospect that at the close of his journey, on the way to the coast, an attack of opthalmia had prevented him from keeping a regular diary, he reassures us that, 'No very remarkable incident . . . occurred in this interval—either medically or socially, except what has been told in the pages of *Darkest Africa*' (p.482).

The reference to Stanley's text, *In Darkest Africa*, points to the transmission of these experiences to the public realm, a movement eased by the descriptions of Parke's (and therefore Western) medical proficiency. The episodes relaying the demonstration of the latter are employed to highlight the bond between the whites whilst emphasising their superiority to and distance from the blacks. So when, for example, the party is attacked by natives at the village of Avisibba and one of Parke's white colleagues, W.G. Stairs, is hit by a poisoned arrow, Parke recounts how he sucked the poison out of the wound for him, but writes of the blacks in the expedition, 'Many of our men were also badly wounded, and were sucked by their comrades' (p.92). No such intimacy is to be permitted here between white and black. (Blood brotherhood, often involving the sucking of another's blood, was a different matter since it was usually, for those whites who performed the ritual with influential blacks, a case of political expediency.)

The racial prejudice and stereotypes justifying this aloofness are upheld in the guise of sanitary considerations. Near the beginning of the expedition, on board the boat the 'Henry Reed', Parke finds that: 'there is but one cabin, and this is occupied during the day by eleven filthy, dirty negresses of Tippu-Tib's harem. I am obliged to occupy this malodorous den by night, so I naturally spend as much time as I can on deck, to get the fresh air' (p.53). The effect is to support popular images of blacks' idleness, indifference and ignorance, through personal experience and the scientific discourse of medicine. As the expedition goes on, ulcers increasingly become a problem. Parke's account of these afflictions again combines medical comment with ascribed racial characteristics:

> the habits of the Zanzibaris are disgustingly filthy. They scrape holes in the floors in which they wash their ulcers; they vomit and expectorate on the floor, and cover the ejecta over with clay. I am occasionally treated to the sight of these creatures putting their food to boil in the pot in which they have washed their ulcers, and without having taken the trouble of washing it well out afterwards, &c., &c.. The starting point of these ulcers is undoubtedly contagion in many cases; this is conveyed by flies, &c., and any part so affected (as by irritation of fly-bites, &c.) immediately becomes the centre of a rapidly spreading ulcer. (p.256)

The diary keeps the self at the centre of the action and of the reader's concerns—'I am occasionally treated to . . .'—with the significance of the other and its surroundings depending upon their encroachment on the diarist's consciousness. Rarely does Parke display any empathy with the sufferings of the blacks, and when he does it is usually with the Zanzibaris in his party rather than with the Africans through whose territory they pass. On one occasion he is even able to narrate how he had been called away to see a child who had fallen from a tree: 'I said it would die; it fulfilled my prognosis, for it was dead at 5 P.M. On the way to see it a much more serious accident occurred to myself; I tore my only pyjamas' (p.132).

The establishment of the primacy of the self acts as an agent for the parallel elevation of middle-class mores. When expressing his moral and professional disgust that a river from which they obtain their drinking water is polluted with the excrement of Africans who wash in the stream, he complains that 'they squat down—men and women together—and act up to their belief that the calls of nature have a prior claim to those of decency' (p.189). Decency, then, is the mantle by which civilised society clothes itself against base nature.

A similar donning of the cloak of civilisation, in this case represented by the uniform of the surgeon and the judiciary, is assumed when Parke notes that he has seen many Wanyamwezi whose hands have been amputated on the orders of Mirambo, king of Unyanyembe, to prevent his prisoners-of-war from fighting him in the future. The lack of elaboration in the reporting underscores the lack of sophistication in the ritual: 'The operation is performed by laying the hand on a board, and chopping it off' (p.473). Readers of journals and narratives of travel in Africa would be familiar with images of mutilation carried out as punishments. Here Parke's writing signals the cultivation of self and Western culture: in Africa, where technology is portrayed as primitive, an 'operation' has a purpose and result opposite to its counterpart in the West. Where some medical knowledge is possessed it is shown as natural rather than acquired. Parke's pygmy Monbuttu woman companion does admit him to the secrets of forest poisons and their antidotes, but her praiseworthy qualities as a nurse—she tends Parke through several bouts of fever—are natural, instinctive, and not the product of education in a worthy society, as Parke cannot help reminding himself and his readers: 'My little pygmy is one of the best of nurses, and would be invaluable as attendant to anyone who had no optic or olfactory organs' (p.446). When he prepares to remove the arrowhead from Stairs' chest, he remarks of the Monbuttu woman: 'if any resuscitating agent, such as ammonia, be required, she can emit a modified form at the shortest notice' (p.292), and when the time comes for what seems to be a genuinely sad parting from her, he opines: 'She was always devoted and faithful to me, and, unlike some other ladies of the Dark Continent, her morals were entirely above suspicion' (p.464). Any medical skills found among the Africans are thus firmly situated within their rude social and physical state. Even when Gaetano Casati, a European who was with Emin Pasha, records in his narrative his astonishment at seeing a skilful operation to relieve a woman's badly swollen hand, he can't do so without asking himself if her apparent indifference is proof that 'negroes are endowed with less sensitiveness to pain?'[5]

Parke's diary illustrates vividly David Arnold's argument that by the close of the nineteenth century, 'Europeans began to pride themselves on their scientific understanding of disease causation and mocked what they saw as the fatalism, superstition and barbarity of indigenous responses to disease'.[6] Parke is usually unable to offer a diagnosis of the Africans' condition without passing a judgement on their degradation which is at once both moral and racial. He pronounces, for instance, that, 'Undoubtedly, the Zanzibaris owe a great deal of their physical ill-being to their timidity and laziness, combined with the customary filthiness of their habits' (p.258). It is but a short step from this position to providing the medical equivalent of the widely held view that Africans were beyond spiritual redemption. The step is duly taken when Parke declares that, 'A sick Zanzibari takes no trouble about himself; in fact, he does not want to recover' (p.343). Blame for lack of improvement having been laid in personal terms, Parke elsewhere in the diary enforces the idea of the Zanzibaris' collective responsibility by attacking what he perceives to be 'one of the shabbiest features of the tribe' (p.264); namely, their custom of deserting any of their number who falls seriously ill.

My point here is that we witness the enablement of the appropriation of human property by means similar to those by which Paul Carter sees land being gained by whites in Australia. Carter argues that whites sought to acquire land on the basis of Aborigines' failure to understand the idea of possession. Thus the whites 'possessed a country of which the Aborigine was unaware. To talk of contracts and boundaries to an Aborigine was to talk a foreign language. Logically then, possession could go ahead without consultation'.[7] In the same sense, Parke represents whites in Africa as having the knowledge to hold power over Africans' bodies while simultaneously achieving control of territory. It is no coincidence that on this expedition Stanley negotiated treaties with a number of chiefs on behalf of the Imperial British East Africa Company.[8] And, after all, the Zanzibaris were employed as porters and to offer military support when required. The dual assumption of land and body applied especially in cases where identity was seen in tribal rather than geographical terms, and where the practice of witchcraft could be played up as a factor.

Parke fully supported the execution of deserters and was himself responsible for numerous beatings of others who neglected their duty as defined by the whites. Thus we can see arising the situation in which, as Frantz Fanon later put it in Algeria: 'the doctor always appears as a link in the colonialist network, as a spokesman for the occupying power', and in which 'Science depoliticised, science in the service of man, is often non-existent in the colonies'.[9]

What we have in Parke's journal is medical science in the service of whites communicated through a literary form, the diary, also in the service of whites. The illness of Parke and his colleagues is rendered a positive force: various charts of weight-losses are just one device for the creation of an ordered pattern in the emerging narrative. Another is the chronological structure of the diary itself which combines with the often faltering and painful, but nevertheless actual, movement of the journey to provide a sense of progression. The development, chronicled on the page day by day, is couched in moral, physical and cultural terms, with the trope of medicine supplying the link. It merely testifies to the arrogance of this discourse and to the continuing developments in the science that we now know Parke's terminology to have been 'very vague, reflecting the state of European medical knowledge at the end of the nineteenth century'.[10]

Similarly, there have been corresponding increases in the level of sophistication of the literary form employed by Parke. However, a more obviously important facet is seen when Parke cares for Stanley through twenty-three days of grave illness. The crisis affecting the white leader of the expedition is afterwards discussed by Stanley himself in language stressing the rewards of a functional and stratified society which will pull together for the preservation of its head (and here we notice that gender roles are emphasised too): 'Dr. Parke has been most assiduous in his application to my needs, and gentle as a woman in his ministrations. For once in my life every soul around me was at my service, and I found myself an object of universal solicitude night and day'.[11] As Parke's medical care saves Stanley, so the imagery used in communicating medical knowledge is designed to strengthen Western society by fostering the impression of a purposeful activity made possible by each component of a hierarchy playing its part. Parke's carefully ordered discourse on bacteriology, in a chapter written after his return to England, illustrates this point in a socio-political metaphor:

> The humblest citizen of the animal kingdom is an undifferentiated cell: the highest is formed of a countless number of these elementary structures, variously modified, and set apart to perform definite functions in their respective positions in the economy; but all descended from a single (and simple) parent cell—the ovum. (p.166)

Parke's exhibition of medical imperialism, if we may so term it, is not limited to the practice of Western medicine and its concomitant negative views of those who hold to other forms. Rather, it is significant that Parke is seen to be able to operate in both systems; to participate in both technologies, even if the Africans' technology is presented more in the guise of a ritual. Thus the doctor records that, 'I had a special surgical operation imposed upon me to-day—the circumcision of Kibori (Nelson's boy), who required this finishing touch to place him on a par with the Zanzibari boys'. The performance of this act enhances the Westerner's power by showing him to be proficient in the two worlds, but it also invests him with an historical authority which he can appear to assume through this incident of entry into the culture of the Other, for he goes on to proclaim that, 'The institution of this Oriental operation reaches to the most remote antiquity, more than 2400 years before the Christian era' (p.257)

The converse of this movement is hardly afforded to the Arabs and

Africans. Parke's perception of them as passive victims (often contributing to their illnesses) reduces them to objects, diminishing the possibility of their asserting or freeing themselves by the acquisition of his knowledge and power. At times they are portrayed as having no consciousness or existence beyond their sickness. And then they are seen as wounding the environment too:

> The men were really in a miserable state from debility and hunger, I never saw so repulsive a sight as that furnished by the unfortunate creatures; eaten up as they are with enormous ulcers. As they came dropping in, the stench—emitted by the putrid flesh and the dirty scraps of bandages—was sickening, and actually filled the air all around the Fort, as well as within it. The great majority of the ulcers were on the lower extremities—great, gangrenous, rapidly-sloughing surfaces most of them—many were up to a foot in length, and about half as wide, with the bone exposed along the whole length. Many had hopelessly destroyed the feet: in some cases the tarsus, metatarsus and phalanges had all dropped out by degrees, and great strings of putrid flesh were left hanging out from the stump. (p.336)

In this passage Parke holds on to his scientific position by his use of the Latin names for the bones, in some contrast to the images and diction of the rest of the section. He can consequently continue to fulfill his function, at the same time offering a cold reminder of the physical decay of those around him: 'This day I removed as much dead bone as could conveniently be packed on two soup plates' (p.336). So, the very occasion of the surgeon's performance is portrayed in terms that delineate his power to act upon his passive patients who are consumed by their own sickness ('eaten up with . . . enormous ulcers'). The mention of his packing the dead bones on to soup plates makes even more remote the chance of him becoming similarly consumed: he has a power over objects and people that is denied to the blacks.

This control is communicated in part through the structure of the diary, for the chronological schema allows him to document any positive developments (though their positive aspects may not become clear in the short-term). For instance, a month earlier than the above passage, he writes:

> I now treat the sloughing, and very chronic ulcers by directly applying pure carbolic acid to the surface. This gives very little pain, and has the effect of causing them to skin over—in a way that every other application had failed to do. (p.300)

His progress is set against the continuing illness of the blacks. On the other hand, ill-health suffered by the white members of the expedition may be depicted in ways that will reflect the comparatively advanced technology of their culture. The reunion with the starving Nelson, 'a living skeleton, with hollow cheeks, sunken eyes, and bearing every trait of the extremest physical depression' moves Parke to represent him as 'a photographic record of the horror, which he has outlived' (p.133). He has survived those horrors and is now distanced from them by the manner of their recording. In that aspect the figure of the photographic record parallels the diary, which likewise bears witness to disease whilst offering a distance from it. When Parke writes his diary entries he cannot, by the very nature of the diary, inscribe an ultimate defeat by disease. Any entry is a testament of life. And in literary terms, the diary as a means of cultural and self-expression is denied to the blacks with and amongst whom the expedition is travelling.

The literary communication of medical practice, then, combines two skills in which the Africans are held to be deficient. Many travellers had told of episodes revealing the superstitious regard with which Africans viewed writing; either seeing it as 'bad medicine' or as a powerful charm that may be used in a positive way. As for 'proper' medicine itself, Sir John Lubbock had stated the position bluntly in his study, *The Origin of Civilisation and the Primitive Condition of Man: Mental and Social Condition of Savages*, in which he declaimed:

> Ignorant as they are of the processes by which life is maintained, of anatomy and of physiology, the true nature of disease does not occur to them. Thus the negroes universally believe that diseases are caused by evil spirits.[12]

The absolute certainty with which it is averred that the 'savages' have no conception of the 'true' nature of disease suggests, I think, an underlying belief on the part of whites in a single, unitary truth, whilst the deriding of the 'negroes'' universal belief in the causation of disease by evil spirits encourages a perception of the diversity of the causes and symptoms of disease, though preferring the faith in the essential truth of the disease. From this reading emerges a systematic construction of singular truth attainable through various approaches. One may readily extend this model to the socio-political sphere, to the functional hierarchy of the British state, in which application it is surely meant to fulfill a conservative role, although it clearly has reference too to the increasing specialisation of medicine in the West, thus acting as a marker of progress. (I think, incidentally, that this need for the duality of the political status quo and advanced technological development is a late nineteenth-century reflection of the requirement a century earlier for a new concept of 'civilisation', noted by Raymond Williams.)[13]

In Parke's diary we have the promotion of capitalism as an agent of the newly varied search for truth. We have evidence of the commodification of the means for treating disease. Of his treatment of Stanley, Parke notes:

> I gave him a hypodermic dose of morphine and atropine at 5 P.M., and repeated this at 9 P.M.; so I am hoping for a much easier night. These medicines are all contained in Burroughs and Welcome's tabloids, which I have found extremely satisfactory; as they are very soluble, while they occupy very little space, and have never lost their strength. I have never used any therapeutic preparations at all so convenient or so reliable. The medical departments of the services should abandon the present clumsy and inconvenient system of carrying fluids, pills, powders, &c., and adopt this mode of administering medicines: as it is safer, the dose is more reliable, and transport so much easier—they occupy less than quarter the space and weight; also one medical officer could attend to four times the number of patients. (pp.201-2)

Not only does Parke, the army medical surgeon, endorse their product, but Burroughs and Welcome come to advertise it on the strength of its service on the expedition. In a sense, I think, the promotion of the product by the individual in some ways authenticates the white self which has the power (unlike the blacks) to administer this form of medical technology. There is a kind of public exchange happening here which inadvertently calls into question certain aspects of the nature of the diary, which were in any case tested more severely by the controversy surrounding two other officers on the expedition, Barttelot and Jameson, whose diaries were published posthumously and, in both cases, edited by relatives of the dead men and interspersed with letters.

Neither diary, it was said, had been intended for publication. Barttelot's brother apologised for the literary style. Jameson's wife assured the reader of her husband's diaries that they were being 'published in what is practically their original form, with only such alterations as their private nature required'. This caveat led to some criticism from commentators who thought they should be published in their entirety if truth were to be seen to be fully told. This raises questions about the function of the diary in private and in public. Jameson's brother confidently pronounced that:

> A man's diary is a self-revelation. His true personality is as certain to present itself continually as the refrain in a theme of music. No man lies to himself, when night after night, as his work is done, he

sits down to write out the story of his life from day to day; and the life which Jameson reveals to us in his Diary is one whose keynote is duty, kindliness, and hard work.

The British code won't recognise here any dissembling (thus exerting considerable pressure to conform to this expectation of standards on diarists whose work may be seen by others). Likewise, for Barttelot's brother, 'the diaries and letters direct from the hands of the dead form evidence of supreme value. . . . They have not been able to alter or to add a tittle to what was written at the time'.[14]

Such a belief in the veracity of the diarist (shared even by those opponents who associated a moral and mental decline with the two men's physical demise) and in the accuracy of his or her descriptions—Stairs wrote in an article, 'The best method of getting an insight to our daily life will perhaps be to give extracts from my journals'—imbues the diary with a restorative quality, by which the self is assured of its recognition by the other.[15] Its author and its observations are given the support of the culture of which they are a reflection. In this case and in this sense the diary itself supplies the literary complement to the medical skills possessed by Parke.

When, at the close of the journey, Parke concludes:

> taking into consideration the privations to which we were subjected during the course of the Expedition, covering a space of three years, I think that its net results point very hopefully to the chances of survival of the white man in Africa. (p.482)

then we see the grafting of the self, medicine and imperialism in the diary.

NOTES

1. David Arnold, 'Introduction: disease, medicine and empire', in David Arnold, ed., *Imperial Medicine and Indigenous Societies* (Manchester, 1988).
2. Thomas Heazle Parke, *My Personal Experiences in Equatorial Africa as Medical Officer of the Emin Pasha Relief Expedition* (London: Sampson Low, Marston & Company Limited, 1891). Further page references appear in the text.
3. Robert Thornton, 'Narrative Ethnography in Africa, 1850-1920: The Creation and Capture of an Appropriate Domain for Anthropology', *Man* 18, 3 (1983), p.505.
4. See Paul Carter, *The Road to Botany Bay: An Essay in Spatial History* (London, 1987).

5. Gaetano Casati, *Ten Years in Equatoria and the Return with Emin Pasha*, trans. Hon. Mrs. J. Randolph Clay, 2 vols. (London, 1891), I, p.251.
6. Arnold, 'Introduction: disease, medicine and empire', p.7.
7. Carter, *The Road to Botany Bay*, p.64.
8. See for example John S. Galbraith, *Mackinnon and East Africa 1878–1895: A Study in the 'New Imperialism'* (Cambridge, 1972).
9. Frantz Fanon, *Studies in a Dying Colonialism*, trans. Haakon Chevalier, with a new introduction by A.M. Babu (London, 1989), pp. 131 and 140. In the context of nineteenth-century Africa, Dorothy Helly reminds us of Livingstone's description of slavery as the 'open sore' in the heart of Africa, 'a metaphor used by Livingstone which captured the dual perspective he brought to Africa as a doctor and a missionary'. The ending of the slave trade would 'make it possible for Africans to live what he as a European envisioned as productive, industrious, and ultimately Christian lives'; Dorothy O. Helly, *Livingstone's Legacy: Horace Waller and Victorian Mythmaking* (Athens, OH, 1987), p.28.
10. Janina Konczacki, 'The Emin Pasha Relief Expedition (1887–1889): Some Comments on Disease and Hygiene', *Canadian Journal of African Studies* 19, 3 (1985), p.619.
11. Henry M. Stanley, *In Darkest Africa: or the Quest, Rescue and Retreat of Emin Governor of Equatoria*, new edition (London, 1893), p.213.
12. Sir John Lubbock, *The Origin of Civilisation and the Primitive Condition of Man: Mental and Social Condition of Savages*, third edition (London, 1875), p.25.
13. Raymond Williams, *Marxism and Literature* (Oxford, 1977), p.13.
14. Mrs. J.S. Jameson, ed., *Story of the Rear Column of the Emin Pasha Relief Expedition by the Late James S. Jameson, Naturalist to the Expedition* (London, 1890); quotations from pp. xiii and xxiii. Walter George Barttelot, ed., *The Life Of Edmund Musgrave Barttelot*, third edition (London, 1890), p.8.
15. Jameson died from fever after allegedly commissioning an act of cannibalistic murder. His own diary records the killing, but claims that he had not meant to solicit the deed. Barttelot was shot by a native after behaviour condemned by many as harshly cruel and prejudiced. W.G. Stairs, 'Shut up in the African Forest', *The Nineteenth Century* XXIX, 167 (January, 1891), p.47.

ANTHONY FOTHERGILL

Of Conrad, Cannibals, and Kin

> Human eyes cannot perceive things but in the shape they know them by.
>
> Montaigne

> Not as she is, but as she fills his dreams
>
> Christina Rossetti

One of the earliest known, possibly the first, European representations of American Indians is a woodcut, believed to be by Johann Froschauer of Augsburg, dating from 1505 (*illus. 7*). It depicts the Tupinamba Indians of coastal Brazil cheerfully eating human remains. An interpretative inscription (apparently added later) introduces what were to become standard attributes of 'the savage'—nakedness, cannibalism, and sexual licence:

> This figure represents to us the people and island which have been discovered by the Christian King of Portugal or by his subjects. The people are thus naked, handsome, brown, well-shaped in body, their heads, necks, arms, private parts, feet of men and women are a little covered with feathers. The men also have many precious stones in their faces and breasts. No one also has anything, but all things are in common. And the men have as wives those who please them, be they mothers, sisters, or friends, therein make they no distinction. They also fight with each other. They also eat each other even those who are slain, and hang the flesh of them in the smoke. They become a hundred and fifty years old. And have no government.[1]

This account of the engraving reveals a great deal about how Europeans perceived 'New World' Indians. Emphasis is placed on their exotic physical appearance, particularly their nakedness, which is taken to be both attractive and a sign of their lack of civilised culture, a state confirmed by their cannibalism. They are therefore subjects ripe for

spiritual improvement. And material exploitation. They are the pos-
sessors and hence the source (for Europeans) of precious wealth. Their
undeveloped sense of property might connote naïveté: they might accept,
in exchange for their treasures, useless gifts, or even allow their treasures
to be forcibly taken from them. At any rate, El Dorado is in the offing.

But for my present purposes, the content of the description is less
crucial than certain characteristic ways of thinking about cultural
'otherness' that structure it. These ways of thinking—or, more precisely,
of representing—affect later literary and ethnographic accounts of the
cultural Other, particularly in the nineteenth century, for they are
profoundly tenacious and pervasive. So much so, that in this regard,
generic distinctions between 'literary' and 'non-literary' ethnographic
writing prove unsustainable, whether on the grounds of imaginative
invention, artistic licence, and writerly effect, on the one hand, or, on
the other, of allegiance to observable fact. Indeed, in later European
perceptions and representations of the non-European (and perhaps in
all cases where the powerful view 'inferior' others), *projection, contradiction*, and *negation* are the dominant modes of definition. All these are in
play in the quoted inscription.

First, it is highly imaginative in what it 'sees' in the picture: old age
and jewels, for example, to take two of the more innocent glosses. Also
remarkable is its impulse to read into the image such abstractions as the
economic, political, and sexual order (or disorder) of the Indians. It is
as if their nakedness (which is itself imagined) is a blank space onto
which the viewer can project meanings: this 'description' is inscription
in a precise sense. But it is also a contradictory inscribing. The Indians
are said to be both naked and covered with feathers; but in the
illustration, everyone is wearing a covering garment below the waist.
Furthermore, the description acknowledges the physical beauty and
attractiveness of the Indians, and at the same time asserts their almost
bestial savagery. This polarising ambivalence can also be sensed in the
references to the social practices it 'sees' illustrated: shared communal
property (laudable or naïve); sexual practices (pleasurably free or
indiscriminate); internecine warfare, cannibalism, and anarchy.

A third feature of the account bears upon the epistemological problem
of knowing and representing the Other. How can we recognise the utterly
alien? Definitions tend to proceed by negation: 'they' is 'not us'. The
means by which we come to know the unknown Other will always be
determined by our own terms of reference, our own horizon of understanding. Even the absolutely alien is always our alien, the negation of
our normality. In this sense any writing of the Other, whether it

38

acknowledges it or not, is a writing from within, a re-inscribing, via negation, of the writer. So, quite characteristically, this commentary on American 'cannibals' defines them in terms of, but in negation to, the self-understanding of the European: they have no government; they do not have the proper notion of marriage and property relations; they do not wear clothes.

Given the would-be originality and freshness of the image and inscription, it is startling to discover that the inscription itself bears an almost word for word resemblance to Amerigo Vespucci's earlier account of New World natives, which offers gruesome 'witness' to cannibalism and salacious depiction of Indian women's sexual licentiousness. And both, in turn, are indebted to Sir John Mandeville's vivid and enormously popular fourteenth-century geographical fantasy, his *Travels in the Indian Ocean*. There, on the island of Lamary,

> [It is] the custom for men and women to go all naked. . . . And they marry there no wives, for all the women are common. . . . And all the land and property also is common, nothing being shut up, or kept under lock, one man being as rich as another. But in that country there is a cursed custom for they eat more gladly of man's flesh than any other flesh.[2]

In other words, the 'original' inscription is already the reproduction of a reproduction of widely circulating ideas and images of the 'savage' Other.

Aside from what the ancestry of the inscription reveals about the currency of perceptions of the 'savage', I would like to take the relationship between inscription and illustration as a sort of allegory, an allegory about the relationship of European to non-European native cultures, which is to say, an allegory about European readings of European representations of native cultures. First, it is crucial to acknowledge that we are dealing with two orders of representation in illustration and text. Though the illustration itself represents (that is, interprets, construes, or imagines) an event, the illustration is in turn re-presented by the text, a further reading. The illustration may in this instance happen to come chronologically prior to its inscription, but it cannot claim an unmediated primacy of authentic realisation, any more than the inscription can. Even to call it, as I did, the first European illustration of the Native American, is to beg serious questions about the nature and language of visual representation. For the illustration also re-presents, from within specific European horizons, an inherited vocabulary of the Other, and the iconographic tradition it draws upon has a history stretching back to antiquity. That is why the engraving could be 'read' by its European audience: it re-cycled and adapted earlier and familiar images of the 'wild man', of lovers' feasts, of families of wild folk and suckling mothers, and, surprisingly, of the Virgin and child.[3] Furthermore, into these could easily be incorporated images from more classical sources, particularly in the centurion-like appearance and military posture of the feather-skirted males. The visual iconography mediates Otherness by means of the familiarly strange. Representation must always be recognisable.

With the inscription, then, we are in the presence of something at least thrice removed from its subject. It is a representation of a representation, a reading of a reading, and it can stand allegorically for what I think confronts us in later accounts of the cultural Other. As ethnographers of the remarkable, we understand ourselves to be looking at, and describing objectively, real African natives, genuine rural beggars, actual city prostitutes; similarly, as readers of ethnographical accounts, we imagine we are in the presence of the authentically represented Other. But a way of looking and understanding, constrained by the limitations of specific cultural interests, has already intervened. Unable to get behind our own language of experience and its informing interests, we deal—by means of projection, contradiction and negation—with versions of the producing culture, not the cultural Other which our representations purportedly reproduce.

But this inevitable displacing of the Other occasionally leaves traces of itself. The strategies of self-deception involved can produce telling effects, which can themselves be read as signs of our complicity. They allow us to read representations of the Other against the grain and so come to recognise the mechanisms of interested cultural reproduction. One such effect is worth remarking upon in this earliest of illustrations of the New World Indian. A feature of the picture omitted from mention in the inscription—presumably because it is considered of only peripheral importance—is in fact crucial to the deceptive strategy of constructing the Other, and it carries an almost allegorical potency. I refer to the Portuguese galleons, sign of the simultaneous presence and absence of the European observer.

If forms of representation are, in a profound sense, politically and culturally interested and overdetermined, then the question of who is doing the looking and representing is vital. This would be true even—indeed, particularly—when the fact of such partial looking is itself erased or understated. Though they are in the picture, the galleons are not immediately implicated in the local scene. The picture seems to be a kind of historical allegory: the Europeans are coming, but they are not yet there. They are the future civilisation about to arrive. They represent the superior European culture which will seek to improve the 'primitive' cultures they encounter. Imminent colonial intervention is suggested —and given the subsequent history of genocide, we know the chief form this intervention took.

But this visual rhetoric of European distance and absence may be seen to perform another function in terms of representation. If the viewer, the European, is absent from the scene of cannibalism and dubious sexual goings-on, then he is not responsible, as it were, for the construction of what is depicted. The scene is 'objectively' observed; indeed, in a sense it is not being observed at all. The picture declares, 'This is how these Indians live; they simply are like this'. By erasing any ostensible viewing presence, the illustration silently denies that it is someone's (interested, construing) re-presenting. But by the same token, this absent presence reveals the picture as a kind of *trompe l'oeil*: the Europeans are not there to see the depravities of the scene; nevertheless they can picture it all in close detail. Hence the vital role of the imagination in depicting the Other: they know what they are going to see before they see it for the first time. So, absolutely central to the project of understanding representations of the Other is the question of the disclosed or undisclosed presence of the 'observer'. How self-conscious is the viewer? How far does the image reveal and problematise the interested relation he or she bears to the 'subjects'?

I want now to consider, as primary instances of reading the Other, two crucial political/literary moments in the nineteenth century: a poem by Wordsworth first written in 1797, in the spirit of early and radical Romanticism, and Conrad's *Heart of Darkness* (1899), written at the climax of Victorian imperialism.

Wordsworth's 'Animal Tranquillity and Decay' is a depiction of an old, impoverished traveller—an 'other', that is, separated from the viewer not by race, time, or space, but by class.

Animal Tranquillity and Decay
 The little hedgerow birds,
 That peck along the road, regard him not.
 He travels on, and in his face, his step,
 His gait, is one expression: every limb,
 His look and bending figure, all bespeak
 A man who does not move with pain, but moves
 With thought.—He is insensibly subdued
 To settled quiet: he is one by whom

All effort seems forgotten; one to whom
Long patience hath such mild composure given,
That patience now doth seem a thing of which
He hath no need. He is by nature led
To peace so perfect that the young behold
With envy, what the Old Man hardly feels.[4]

The confidence of knowing this other from a poorer social class—and speaking for him—is evident in Wordsworth's rendering.[5] My interest in looking at it is threefold. First, its strategies for reading the Other are almost programatically clear and in interesting ways resemble elements in the illustration I have discussed. Second, in conspicuous rhetorical moves, the poem reveals motifs and modes of representation which, I would argue, are exported later on in the century, re-surfacing in presentations of the ethnic Other which we can witness in such writers as Conrad. Third, by choosing as an example a representation of an Other ostensibly from within the 'same' culture, we are provided with a test-case for asking where Otherness starts. The ethnocentricity which lets us readily locate the Other *over there*, also presumes a unified 'us'; for the obverse side of the coin of Otherness is the interested assumption of community and identity. Are we, in reflecting on the ethnography of cultural otherness, in fact discussing the poetics, hermeneutics, and politics of an alterity of a much more pervasive and radical sort? In short, does alterity begin at home?

For Wordsworth, it can begin in a country lane. Noteworthy, first, is the absence of an ostensible viewer of the old man travelling (as the poem was originally called). In a sense his actions and appearance carry their own unproblematic meaning. He doesn't need to speak, either, for his physical appearance 'bespeaks' his nature and history. I am not saying the description is devoid of any interpreting presence: the use of 'seems' posits a perceiving consciousness. But the identity of this consciousness —and thus any ideological predisposition it has—remains undisclosed and easily ignored. The unostentatious erasing of the viewer, the very anonymity of the presentation, confers authority and objectivity on the meanings attributed to the old man's appearance: he simply *is* like this.

Corroborating this claim to objective authenticity is another linguistic feature, the tense which the poem adopts. Let us call it the tense of the 'ethnographical present', the use of which is remarkably widespread in non-imaginative anthropological texts. The 'ethnographical present' is a writing effect which asserts not temporality and (changing) history but the timeless Now, which is also an eternal past: is and ever was. There is in this regard a poignant parallel to be drawn with the inscription to the Tupinamba representation and its authoritative present tense. Typical of the accounts which circulated very widely in sixteenth-century Europe, often in heavily plagiarised versions, it used the ethnographical present tense to solidify and perpetuate as 'fact' the (privileged) perceptions of witness. Such accounts became the source of anthropological 'knowledge' about the American Indians, particularly their culinary habits, right down to the 1970s, when, centuries after their eradication, Tupinamba cannibalism was still being cited in the 'scientific' ethnographical present tense.[6]

Both these formal aspects of the representation of the old man—the absence of a construing (and limited) consciousness, and the tense—contribute significantly to the meanings his body is said to articulate. The tense evokes the sense of monumentality, a 'thereness', which the figure possesses. (The abstract title and the 'traditional' sonnet form add to this impression of permanence.) His meaning, the solidity of his patient presence as a type and symbol of eternity, is not just stated; it is stylistically guaranteed and reinforced. The interpenetration of body and surroundings transforms him into his meaning: he is enviable animal tranquillity, a vivid moral allegory for those who might see him. Any particularity has been transcended, the physical has become the abstract, pain has become thought. The temporal dimension is one not of social or cultural but of natural history, and he exists in a location barely this side of the human. Thank goodness he does not break the silence with speech. As one critic puts it, 'the total aspect of the old man perfectly "bespeaks" his condition. He does not need to do or say anything—he is'. To which another, concurring, has added, 'One might go further and say that Wordsworth's old man could not have spoken. . . . [His] peace is that of the impervious natural world'.[7]

But the old man does speak in two earlier versions we have of the poem. And Wordsworth's gradual editorial silencing of the old man from the first *Lyrical Ballads* version of 1798, via its emended form of 1805, to this final text of 1815, tells as dramatic a story about construing and representing the Other as the old man's words do about his own experience. Even the change in title is significant. The final version omits the first three and the last two words from the original 'Old Man Travelling; Animal Tranquillity and Decay, A Sketch' (1798)—thus erasing the human and historically particular—and translates the figure into an eternal present of abstract value. Even more disruptive of this picture of passivity are his words, reported in these additional lines in the original:

—I asked him whither he was bound, and what
The object of his journey; he replied
'Sir! I am going many miles to take
A last leave of my son, a mariner,
Who from a sea-fight has been brought to Falmouth,
And there is dying in an hospital.—'

The man's own story, though still restrained in the telling by his awareness of the social distance from his interlocutor ('Sir'), nevertheless offers to the reader a powerful competing reading. His words reveal a personal (and cultural and political) history which profoundly belies the meanings the observing 'I'—now syntactically and socially located in the poem—claimed his appearance 'bespake'. When the old man speaks for himself, he is inserted back into history (note the significant shift to the past tense), and all at once his previous 'meaning' becomes problematic, as does the narrator's claim to know and adequately represent him. The embarrassed confrontation with an alternative account of the old man reveals that the first reading was precisely that—an interested interpretation. (As Oscar Wilde put it, perceptively, of Wordsworth, 'He found in the stones the sermons he had already hidden there'.) This awkwardness was apparently too great, both poetically and politically, for Wordsworth. His editorial erasures silence the old man as they consolidate the meaning projected onto him, mildly composing him, as it were, into a complacent image of otherness as natural passivity. Any resistance to or escape from meaning is thus denied. The old man is construed through negations (he is not regarded, he does not move with pain, he has no need for patience), the piling on of which might, with the benefit of knowing the poem's early versions, smack of protesting too much. The negation of the old man corresponds to the purposes and meanings of those he is not.

So the Other always 'means', does not need to speak for him or herself, has a timeless value which erases particularity and difference, and is accommodated into a moral economy which serves the needs of those for whom he or she is Other. The Other is, in short, a construction of the viewing observer, even and particularly when the act of viewing is itself understated.

The potency of the images used to represent nineteenth-century impoverished classes (descendants of Wordsworth's old man) proved to be transportable. It has been pointed out that many of the same stereotypes employed in the depiction of the Dark Continent found fertile ground in the imaginations of the Victorian reader already used to portrayals of the English poor.[8] Just as explorers had ventured forth in the 'discovery' of Africa (as if it had not already been long found by its indigenous populations), so writers in Britain had been exploring the 'unknown' cities of industrial England to discover the exotic and dramatic but nevertheless containable Other in the form of the working class. The climates of the two locations might be different, but modes of representation do not recognise national boundaries.

Conrad's intervention in late Victorian literature and its representations of the African 'Other' was characteristically complex. He was a writer of his time—indeed, it is difficult to imagine what it would seriously mean to say the opposite of any writer. But I am not evincing his work simply as an exemplary compendium of all the common stereotypes of Victorian Empire. True, he won early recognition and was published by W.E. Henley in the Tory and jingoistic pages of the *New Review*. Henley saw him as one of his regatta, a comrade-in-arms for the literature of imperialist gusto and masculine heroics. But dismissing any comparisons with Kipling, Rider Haggard, and R.L. Stevenson, Conrad saw himself using romance genre forms, but very much for his own ends. He was a writer living culturally at the margins. A foreign sailor coming late to writing (in his third language), a Pole whose nationalism was borne under the yoke of imperialism (Russian), not in the name of it, Conrad stood both inside and outside popular Victorian culture. He knew and could exploit its vocabulary and ways of seeing—but use them aslant. His marginality lent him the capacity to view the culturally familiar with an estranged eye. Thus he did not simply absorb and unproblematically reiterate the ideological predispositions of his time. Rather, he could re-present their forms to 'make us see' their hidden terms, to quote his Preface to *The Nigger of the Narcissus*.

Heart of Darkness provides us with a seminal version of such representation, but one which, I will argue, demonstrates both the culmination of a nineteenth-century literary/political way of seeing the Other and an inherent and radical critique of its own assumptions. In that respect, the novel can be regarded as prefiguring some of the most significant developments in later twentieth-century analyses of cultural representation. But to recognise the self-critique for what it is, we need first to acknowledge the degree to which Conrad was articulating very persistent and widely circulating cultural stereotypes. These profoundly influenced the Europeans' way of looking at and comprehending their first encounter with Africa. The representation of the Other, particularly when it foregrounds such attributes as the exotic, the utterly different, the alien—in short, the original—is anything but original.

Recent studies have done much to uncover the cultural assumptions underpinning anthropological and literary representations of nineteenth- and twentieth-century Africa. H. Alan Cairns and Philip Curtin have sought to establish not so much the history of European cultural contacts with Africa, as a history of the European representations of these contacts, that is, the images and frames of reference through which the European perceived 'the African'. My way of putting this—the very use of the monolithic, generalising abstraction 'the African'—implies an elemental being true through all time and space, essentially devoid of historical or cultural specificity. The term itself is a symptom of the problematics of representation which this essay seeks to address. And if it is validly objected that 'the European' is equally false as a category, since it also asserts an ahistorical homogeneity, then I would say that it is false—but not equally false. It should be remembered that binary terms (European/African, Civilised/Primitive) are never used with im- partial and balanced interest. It is only a trick of apparent linguistic symmetry which conceals the fact that the opposition itself is generated by the language of one of the two sides of the opposition, the side which has particular conative values at play and power interests at stake in the evocation.

Speaking of pioneers whose religious or trade interests prescribed their writing, Cairns summarises the mid-Victorian perception of Africa thus:

> By and large these pioneers saw little of virtue in African cultures. Their observations, usually biased, frequently contradictory, and often simply wrong, are replete with danger to the uncritical research worker. In almost all the nineteenth-century books on Africa the figure of the white man is writ large on the African landscape. In the middle of the dark continent he assumes novel and grandiose proportions. In moral, spiritual, and technological matters he appears as a giant among pygmies, dwarfing the Africans among whom his activities are carried out.[9]

A supplementary argument but a crucial one in the present context is offered by Curtin, who says that even by the 1850s an imagery of Africa reproduced in travel and missionary writing was well publicised and firmly established in the European mass-circulation media.

> It was found in children's books, in Sunday School tracts, in the popular press. Its major affirmations were the 'common knowledge' of the educated classes. Thereafter, when new generations of explorers or administrators went to Africa, they went with a prior

impression of what they would find. Most often they found it, and in their writings in turn confirmed the older image—or at most altered it only slightly.[10]

In other words, anybody going to Africa for the first time had in a sense already been there and was, consciously or not, a carrier of cultural luggage containing well-established assumptions, expectations, and imaginative constructions of 'the African', with which to experience the continent and its peoples, supposedly at first hand.

The latter half of the nineteenth century saw a phenomenal increase in literature dealing with Africa—novels and journals with mass circulation, missionary reports, and scientific accounts. Learned societies such as the Anthropological Society of London (established in 1863 as a separatist group from within the Ethnological Society as a result of the anti-slavery sentiments aroused during the American Civil War) encouraged the developing study of 'primitive' peoples. Added stimulus to the enterprise was given by the perceived cultural implications of Darwin's theory of evolution and by the archaeological discoveries made in the wake of colonial expansion in 1870s and the 1880s. All this contributed a growing body of 'scientific knowledge' about the African, which reinforced even as it modified the terms of earlier literary representations. Growing commercial and political contact (pre-dating the Scramble for Africa but massively increased by it) kindled, in the popular imagination, an infectious interest in the area and in the potent representations of Africa and 'primitive' man which such literature propagated. Furthermore, World Exhibitions such as the Great Exhibition of 1851 at Crystal Palace, and the Paris World Exhibition, as well as other exhibitions run by ethnological societies, were enormously popular and influential, reinforcing a heavily mediated, profoundly stereotypic understanding of foreign 'races'.

The literary and popular imagery in representations of Africa and the African did not remain static, then, despite the persistence of earlier constructions. Like a landscape whose underlying geological formation abides as a traceable determinant but whose surface appearance alters subtly over time, basic structures of understanding Africa and the African Other, premised on Eurocentric fears, desires, and assumed superiority, adapted themselves to new colonial impulses. In particular, the view of Africa as virgin land ripe for economic exploitation in the last decades of the century affected the way the continent and its peoples were represented. For the material interests of the colonialists (which required venture capital investment in profitable enterprises) did not always coincide with the interests and ways of looking which had preoccupied other earlier Europeans in Africa. These had generated images of an exotic, mysterious, and challenging landscape which needed taming (by the intrepid explorer) and of a primitive people who needed converting from heathen beliefs (by missionaries). But an increasing imperialist interest saw the native population less as convertible savages and more as malleable inferiors to be subjugated and controlled as a labour resource.[11]

Given these shifts, let us consider the 'common knowledge' propagated by literary works of the period in order to locate the tradition into which Conrad inserted himself. Here is a fairly typical depiction of the Congolese African of the sort available to Conrad, in this case written by one of the age's 'spiritual fathers', P.P. Aurogard:

> The black race is certainly the race of Ham, the race cursed of God. There is nothing in particular which shows you this, but one can smell it, see it everywhere, and one cannot help feeling both compassion and terror when one sees these poor unfortunates. These black pagans are lazy, greedy, thieves, liars and given over to all kinds of vice. The picture is not a flattering one, but it does not express the whole truth, and the scanty clothes which these unfortunates wear make them even more savage and worthy of pity.[12]

In its characteristic self-assurance, its mixed motivation (the savage must be both utterly beyond redemption and pitiable enough for funds to be contributed for his spiritual welfare), and its unintentional self-contradiction (nothing shows you this, but it can be seen), this account manages acrobatics of an almost metaphysical complexity.

Summing up such stereotypical representations, Hammond and Jablow emphasise that an unequivocally accepted racial determinism underlay all European descriptions of Africans of the period. Earlier polygenist views of the separate origin and species of Africans, according to which European races were inherently more developed and hierarchically superior, eventually gave way before the Darwinian monogenist theory of human evolution. But in the later decades of the century, popularised versions of Darwin were used to reconfirm, in difference, the white man's racial and cultural superiority. Evolutionary inferiority then became the enabling ground for the perception of the African as a beastly, and time-locked, savage. In Africa, it could be asserted, the European was in the presence of the contemporary primitive. Physical ugliness, non-individuated uniformity of appearance, excessive sexual appetite, and promiscuity are recurrent motifs in descriptions of these 'primitive' people. A host of mental and moral failings were alleged to reinforce the fact of Africans' social and cultural backwardness:

> They were ignorant as well as incapable of any intellectual attain-
> ment. They lacked any sense of time; they couldn't think in abstract
> terms; since they were without the gifts of invention or creativity,
> they were innately imitative . . . [Emotionally unstable, they lacked]
> all the finer feelings such as gratitude, pity, or true love. Morally .
> . . they were lazy, liars, thieves, cowards and bullies.[13]

An inevitable, permanent, and essential gulf separated white colonisers from their African subjects—rationalisation enough for the imperial and racial interests of the Europeans. So, the eighteenth-century convention of the noble savage was out, and the ignoble savage was in? Not quite. The latter overlaid but did not eradicate the former. The stereotypic construction of the 'noble savage', quite as unhistorical as that of the later 'contemporary ancestors', fed a cultural and political interest in the natural and the exotic which was fostered by the Romantics and subsequent nineteenth-century writers and painters, particularly in France, in the work of Baudelaire, Nerval, Flaubert, and the immensely popular Pierre Loti. The imaginative function of the African landscape and its inhabitants as exotic Other (thoroughly exploited in the volumi-nous travel literature of the period) was twofold. On the one hand it represented an impulse of flight from aspects of the dominant European bourgeois industrial culture. It was an imaginative space to be escaped into; or one from which bourgeois Europe could be criticised. On the other hand, confronting the strange and the unfamiliar held out the promise of self-discovery. Stripped of its repressive European veneer of social mores and pretense, the authentic self waited for discovery in the landscape of Africa. Thus, the 'savage' Other could embody the freedom that Europeans desired in order to find their 'real' selves.

These uses of the imagined Africa and the 'savage', though to some extent superseded by later political and cultural requirements during the period of imperial expansion, were never quite erased. They continued to play an informing part in the discourse of the Other which Conrad assimilated. It was a discourse predicated upon a structure of opposites. The 'savage' was to be defined against what the perceiving Europeans understood themselves to be. The Other was negation: nature, animal, black. How these attributes were then evaluated de-pended on the needs to which the construction was put. In this economy of oppositions, desire and transgression are in close alliance. But the transgression most to be feared was the transgression of 'known' boundaries. Paradoxically, Westernised Africans came to be regarded as particularly threatening, for they confused and disrupted the supposed natural order.

It is into this context that we should place Conrad's *Heart of Darkness*, for it draws heavily on the most pervasive and contradictory nineteenth-century European images of the African, even when it seeks to reevaluate them. The argument I would like to offer is that there exists in Conrad's representation of the African a radically ambivalent tendency. At times his representation endorses stereotypic figures of the 'savage' Other, even when the aim of the endorsement is apparently to question facile assertions of the opposition between (superior) Civilised and (inferior) Savage. At other times, his representation of the African Other offers a critique of European representations, even to the point of questioning the very basis of such 'otherness'. Broadly speaking, instances of the two tendencies vary according to the proximity or distance of the narrator (Marlow) from the subject of his observation.[14] In other words, when Marlow specifies the African subject's historical or political context, the representation tends to be critical of typical European representations. When Marlow erases the specific context, the representation tends to endorse the stereotype.

Proximity alone, however, is no guarantee of clear sight. It *can* facilitate one of two challenges to stereotypical representation. The first seeks to undermine the idea of the culturally constructed Other altogether. Distance and unfamiliarity, so the argument goes, provide a breeding ground for false cultural stereotypes which rely on the perpetuation of a notion of difference as natural, inherent and unchangeable. The experience gained through proximity and social interaction can therefore lead to a denial of any significant difference at all. This easy identification runs a real risk of concealing its sources—the observer's own cultural assumptions, projected onto another—and thus continues to deny alterity to the Other.

But proximity can offer a more powerful, if more modest, challenge to the process of stereotyping precisely by exposing the processes and forms of representation. This second form of challenge seeks to highlight, to put in quotation marks, as it were, the representations hitherto offered as disinterested 'descriptions' of the Other, to recognise their cultural pedigree and the historical and material interests which all representations involve. The significance of Conrad lies not in his capacity to reflect the ideological predispositions of his cultural situation (which most nineteenth-century representations of Africa managed to achieve) but in his ability to re-present them in such a way that his work, often despite appearances, reinvestigates the *terms* of representation for the purpose of self-critique.

Two pivotal episodes in the novel can be seen as revealing the tension between endorsement and critique in Conrad: the appearance of the chain-gang soon after Marlow arrives in the Congo, and his subsequent up-river journey. The latter includes his confrontation with what he perceives as the threatening mystery of the forest and its inhabitants, culminating in his arrival at Kurtz's Inner Station encampment and the appearance of Kurtz's black mistress. However, before looking at the incidents in detail, we might consider two of the terms I've just used, 'the Congo' and 'Kurtz's mistress'. Both of these almost incidental turns of phrase reveal significant but more or less unconscious contaminations of language by stereotypic assumptions. Neither phrase is used in *Heart of Darkness*, yet how easily we slip into them. There is, in fact, no reference in the novel to an exact geographical setting, though our knowledge of Conrad's own trip up the River Congo allows us to gloss over this. Indeed, the lack of reference can be justified textually by suggesting that in his work Conrad adopts a geographical and historical anonymity to extend the range of the themes he is engaging. He does not want the experience he narrates to be felt to have only limited application. But the erasure of precise location and of historical and ethnic specificity gives to the native peoples he represents the appearance of the near-mythic. We are given 'natural man' stripped of the accoutrements of social reality, in formal qualities very like Wordsworth's old man: eternally present; at one with nature; and offering some kind of lesson to 'us'. The translation into 'primitive man' becomes all the easier if we are not preoccupied with the specificities of the later nineteenth-century Congo but can let our imaginations freely inscribe the blank space the Other has become. We will need to return presently to the complex erotic component of this blankness in the representation of the doubly Other, the 'savage' female.

Less problematic for the cultural climate in which Conrad was writing is this representation of African natives:

> Going up that river was like travelling back to the earliest beginnings of the world, when vegetation rioted on the earth and the big trees were kings. An empty stream, a great silence, an impenetrable forest. . . . We were wanderers on the prehistoric earth, on an earth that wore the aspect of an unknown planet. We could have fancied ourselves the first men taking possession of an accursed inheritance, to be subdued at the cost of profound anguish and of excessive toil. But suddenly, as we struggled round a bend there would be a glimpse of rush walls, of peaked grass-roofs, a burst of yells, a whirl of black limbs, a mass of hands clapping, of feet stamping, of bodies swaying, of eyes rolling under the droop of heavy and motionless foliage. The steamer toiled along slowly on the edge of a black and

incomprehensible frenzy. The prehistoric man was cursing us, praying to us, welcoming us—who could tell? We were cut off from the comprehension of our surroundings: we glided past like phantoms, wondering and secretly appalled, as sane men would before an enthusiastic outbreak in a madhouse. . . . The earth seemed unearthly. We are accustomed to look upon the shackled form of a conquered monster, but there—there you could look at a thing monstrous and free. It was unearthly, and the men were—No, they were not inhuman. Well, you know, that was the worst of it—this suspicion of their not being inhuman. It would come slowly to one. They howled and leaped, and spun, and made horrid faces; but what thrilled you was just the thought of their humanity—like yours—the thought of your remote kinship with this wild and passionate uproar. Ugly. Yes, it was ugly enough: but if you were man enough you would admit to yourself that there was in you just the faintest trace of a response to the terrible frankness of that noise, a dim suspicion of there being a meaning in it which you—you so remote from the night of the first ages—could comprehend. . . . I made out, deep in the tangled gloom, naked breasts, arms, legs, glaring eyes,—the bush was swarming with human limbs in movement, glistening, of bronze colour.[15]

In narrative terms the journey is one of advance towards Kurtz with echoes of Stanley's search for Livingstone (as a sort of Holy Grail, a narrative with immense resonance in the popular mind). It is represented as a journey of return, through a landscape as primordial as 'the night of the first ages'. The long forgotten becomes the present; the prehistoric becomes the here and now. The formal qualities of the passage, particularly the use of the iterative past tense suggesting repeated, habitual actions ('we would', 'there would be') make time seem to turn back on itself. The iterative tense perfectly mirrors the sense of time suspended. Furthermore, topography and inhabitants merge into one another. Like Wordsworth's old man travelling, though with obvious evaluative differences, these natives are absorbed into the natural, and located in a virtually dehistoricised space. The human body is expressed as an unindividuated mass of limbs; human speech is reduced to 'incomprehensible frenzy'; and the wilderness is given anthropomorphic qualities—it has the power to look, it has inscrutable purposes—at the moment when the historical, social human is all but erased. The 'prehistoric' both is and is not in historical time.[16] And the human 'primitive', 'prehistoric man', transgresses the border of established oppositional categories, such as human/non-human, sane/insane, human/animal, in a way which, as we have seen, both horrifies and fascinates Marlow when he questions 'their not being inhuman'.

The account Marlow gives and the thematic thrust of much of the novel radically disturb the complacent sense of European superiority which Marlow's listeners, and Conrad's contemporary readers, would in all likelihood have shared. That 'civilised' behaviour may be just a veneer covering aggressive, passionate, incomprehensible energies was a fear too current to be comfortably dismissed. But in order to articulate it, Conrad needed to construct the black as an objectification of what it was they were anxious about. Thus, both a radical critical and a racist reactionary force are engaged in this use of the stereotypical representation of the African Other, a representation which simultaneously confirms while undercutting the European cultural myth of the black as a contemporary ancestor. The culturally and politically dominant reading of this myth was imperially complacent: we too were once like this, but how developed we can see ourselves to be now (in comparison)! But, with a different Darwinian turn, Conrad has also articulated the underlying fear: if we came from this, what secret inheritance may be lurking in our characters? (One can almost hear the class anxieties about having come from lowly stock.) But in either case the stereotype remains intact.

The same combination of fear and desire can be located in the depiction of the 'wild and gorgeous apparition of a woman', Kurtz's native mistress, as she is universally called in Conrad criticism. The appellation 'mistress' itself reveals a different order of stereotyping at work. For nowhere in the narrative itself is the black woman referred to as Kurtz's mistress; it is a status inferred from the text. It is probable that neither for Marlow nor his listeners, nor for Conrad's implied readers, could the logic of this inferred stereotype be fully articulated. Nor would it need to be so articulated. As an unspoken 'truth' it is always already known that the black native woman in nineteenth-century European narratives means sexual licence. The connotations are activated by a cultural system (with its assumptions about racial difference) which confirms the black as 'passionate' and 'sexually active' and the black woman, specifically, as embodying physical temptation and the source of sexual gratification for the white male European. Like the representation of American Indians in the sixteenth century, the comparative nudity of the African woman was read as clear testimony of her transgressive sexuality. The power of the stereotype lies in its self-evidence, as the compliance of most of Conrad's twentieth-century critics testifies. What fascinated and terrified the colonising mind was the thought that the white man might 'go native' (a euphemism for crossing the limits of the permissible) and undermine the sexual cornerstone of the bourgeois world.

The phrase 'wild and gorgeous apparition' reinforces Marlow's oxymoronic definition of the wilderness (the unearthly earth) and expresses within the stereotyping a deep ambivalence: utterly other and incomprehensible, it is nevertheless and therefore fascinatingly attractive. Her 'barbarous' beauty replaces the horrid faces and monstrous appearance of the natives, but she shares their absorption into the natural. An incarnation of its seductive and potentially corrupting force, she stands at one with and undifferentiated from the wilderness. She is its image, its soul. Her well-armoured appearance evokes the familiar Amazonian stereotype, a powerful female threat to the male, but this is given an emphasis of tragic dignity and sorrow. Victim, like the wilderness, of the European invasion, she also threatens to be its vanquisher. As an 'apparition' (a telling word in the light of her evident physical presence, when 'figure' or 'appearance' might have worked as well), her status in reality is brought into question, as well it might be. She shares the 'unearthliness' of the earth: she is seen to occupy a space on the borderline between the real and the unreal, the human and the non-human, the material and the fantastic—an impossible position. For all her physicality, she is indeed an apparition. She functions as an imaginative space onto which Marlow can inscribe the meanings and desires of the European male gaze, while at the same time these inscriptions can be passed off as the inherent qualities of the object gazed at. The European can then 'discover' his kinship and fascination for what he has projected onto her. But of course the inscribing is not declared. Although the woman is being looked at, the meanings of the depiction are attributed not to the viewer but to the viewed. We are, it seems, back to Wordsworth-like strategies of seeing the Other.

There is, moreover, a silencing here reminiscent of Wordsworth's silencing of the old man travelling. We hear about her speaking, but we do not hear her words. Like the monstrous natives, she is not allowed to come close enough to speak for herself, to appropriate her own verbal space. If her political space has been colonised, so has her linguistic one. Narratively, she has to be held at arm's length, only to be represented, spoken for, by Marlow and the Russian Harlequin. Thus the ideological work of the representation can go on unhindered by the entry into the historical and specific, into the closer space of contestation and real difference which her talking may reveal. Instead, her 'inscrutable' and hence threatening 'purposes' are registered in a displaced phallic response on the part of the Russian Harlequin:

She turned away slowly, walked on, following the bank, and passed

into the bushes to the left. Once her eyes gleamed back at us in the
dusk of the thickets before she disappeared.

'If she had offered to come aboard I really think I would have tried
to shoot her,' said the man of patches, nervously. (p.101)

There are two instances, however, where proximity and contact go some
way toward contesting the stereotyping of the Other which the novel
elsewhere depends on: the depictions of the chain-gang and the cannibal
crew. The physically precise description of the former, with its emphasis
on detail and its withholding of the term 'chain-gang' until the condition
of the natives' bodily presence has been established, shocks the reader
into a fresher recognition of the event. Made impressionistically aware
of the sheer physicality of the 'chain-gang', the word itself is de-
familiarised. The process of signification—and what is at stake in it—is
held up for scrutiny.

A slight clinking behind me made me turn my head. Six black men
advanced in a file, toiling up the path. They walked erect and slow,
balancing small baskets full of earth of their heads, and the clink
kept time with their footsteps. Black rags were wound round their
loins, and the short ends behind waggled to and fro like tails. I could
see every rib, the joints of their limbs were like knots in a rope; each
had an iron collar on his neck, and all were connected together with
a chain whose bights swung between them, rhythmically clinking.
Another report from the cliff made me think suddenly of that ship
of war I had seen firing into a continent. It was the same kind of
ominous voice; but these men could by no stretch of imagination
be called enemies. They were called criminals, and the outraged law,
like the bursting shells, had come to them, an insoluble mystery
from the sea. All their meagre breasts panted together, the violently
dilated nostrils quivered, the eyes stared stonily uphill. (pp.42-3)

Conrad's point here has to do with the nature and politics of linguistic
representation: 'They were called criminals'; 'They were not enemies,
they were not criminals'. The 'outraged law' (the phrase *and* the
institution) is exposed to polemical critique: the real outrage may be the
Law's representing the black as criminal. If we call the Other by certain
names, we can legitimise our behaviour towards 'it' accordingly. Everything depends on who is doing the looking. What is the relative power
status of the representer? Who determines the way of looking, the terms
of the representing? However fleetingly, Marlow brings home this
concern when, walking close to the chain-gang, he thinks of himself as
being looked at:

They passed within six inches, without a glance, with that complete,
deathlike indifference of unhappy savages. Behind this raw matter

one of the reclaimed, the product of the new forces at work, strolled despondently, carrying a rifle by its middle. He had a uniform jacket with one button off, and seeing a white man on the path, hoisted his weapon to his shoulder with alacrity. This was simple prudence, white men being so much alike at a distance that he could not tell who I might be. He was speedily reassured, and with a large, white, rascally grin, and a glance at his charge, seemed to take me into partnership in his exalted trust. After all, I also was a part of the great cause of these high and just proceedings.

Instead of going up, I turned and descended to the left. My idea was to let that chain-gang get out of sight before I climbed the hill. (p.43)

He imagines what it might be like to be looking from the Other's viewpoint. Of course, he cannot naively and unpolitically adopt the Other's position, and the fact that they don't give him a glance indicates his separation from them as a European master. But the rascally grin and glance of the native guard, and the joke about white men all looking the same, which inverts the cliché and thus again defamiliarises, works to explode stereotypic European generalisations about 'the black man'. And Marlow feels identified as accomplice in the horror he witnesses. No wonder he wants the chain-gang 'out of sight'. True, he is still projecting a way of looking on to the Other; that is inescapable. But the stereotyping is fractured at the point when he locates himself temporarily in the site of the viewed. He thereby recognises the dialectics of viewing and representing; he is forced to acknowledge that his own historical, political position implicates him. Like Wordsworth's earlier awkwardness when his position (or way of looking) is even mildly contested, Marlow is no longer so keen to see or be seen. His (unsuccessful) form of erasure is to walk off into the grove. There, unfortunately for him (Conrad's political honesty here is uncompromising), he sees more evidence of the results of European well-meaning: cast-off and dying members of the chain-gang. For Marlow—and this is what Conrad is radically, consciously, showing us—the Other has come too close for comfort.

Similar proximity and realignment of perspective occur with the cannibals on the steamer. It is in an offhand sort of way that Marlow introduces the reference: 'Fine fellows—cannibals—in their place', but it nonetheless confounds the stereotype he has just encouraged in depicting those natives on shore. The attributes of 'frenzied passion' and exotic culinary habits are ones with which our complicit imaginations willingly toy. Cannibalism has been the stock-in-trade of European inscriptions of the non-European Other since Herodotus, and it

epitomizes categorical transgression. Conrad surely evokes the cannibalistic attributes as an expected feature of the adventure stories of
Darkest Africa, but the stereotype gets undermined by Marlow's simple
praise of the 'cannibals': 'They were men one could work with and I'm
grateful to them' (p. 67). The restraint they show under attack (compared
to the Europeans' panic) and their surprising reticence to eat portly
European managerial flesh, despite their meagre rations, are qualities
commented on by Marlow in an approving manner. Conrad knows his
audience well enough to evoke the stereotypic cannibal reference—
ubiquitous, indeed almost compulsory, in late nineteenth-century 'descriptions' of Africa, despite a complete lack of any firm evidence for its
widespread existence.[17] But he does so to imply that, with close social
and physical contact, the stereotype dissolves, or rather is itself held up
for critical linguistic and therefore political scrutiny.

In this sort of proximity the 'otherness' of the Other is not denied as
such. What is contested is the complacent idea that 'I already know' the
Other; and that it is my place and my right, as if disinterestedly, to do
the representing. The recognition of proximity is not a sentimental or
self-serving claim to identity. Nor can we claim to get behind our own
understanding to adopt an allegedly neutral position of viewing the
Other 'just as it is'. But we *can* be alerted to the degree to which our
own projective imaginations, our own contradictions, seek to make of
the Other the negative image of ourselves.

NOTES

1. See illustration source, Bayerische Staatsbibliothek, Mnchen, cat. no. Einb.
   V.2, and W. Eames, 'Description of a Wood Engraving Illustrating the
   South American Indians (1505)', *Bulletin of the New York Public Library*
   Vol. 26 (1922), pp.755-60. Illustration also cited and discussed in Hugh
   Honour, *The New Golden Land: European Images of America from the
   Discoveries to the Present Time* (New York, 1975), p.12, and William C.
   Sturtevant, 'First Visual Images of Native America', in F. Chiapelli (ed.),
   First Images of America (Berkeley, 1976), Vol.I, pp.417-54.
2. M.C. Seymour (ed.), *Mandeville's Travels* (Oxford, 1967), pp.131-2. See
   also Frederick Pohl, *Amerigo Vespucci* (New York, 1944), pp.114-6.
3. For the common currency of such 'wild man' images see especially Timothy
   Husband, *The Wild Man: Medieval Myth and Symbolism* (New York, 1980).
4. *Poetical Works of William Wordsworth*, ed. E. de Selincourt and H.
   Darbishire (Oxford, 1940-9), Vol. IV, p.247.
5. The tradition of a fully confident reading of the social Other has a history

stretching back to Plato's *Republic*. In Book IX he adopts a body/mind analogy to assert that the rational man can know and speak for the manual worker; indeed, can do so better than the worker himself:

> To ensure that people of this type [the slave] are under the same authority as the highest type, we have said that they should be subjected to that highest type, which is governed by its divine element; but this control is not exercised, as Thrasymachus thought, to the detriment of the subject, but because it is better for every creature to be under the control of divine wisdom. That wisdom and control should, if possible, come from within; failing that it must be imposed from without, in order that, being under the same guidance, we may all be friends and equals.

The body/slave cannot know itself and cannot therefore fully control itself. However, a system of knowledge and control is necessary to guarantee psychic and social harmony. Thank goodness, therefore, that this can be entrusted to the wise man, who can know and represent to himself the slave's own nature and needs. The underlying political assumption here is of an achievable harmony which nevertheless endorses a hierarchy of knowledge and power. 'Those who cannot know and represent themselves must be represented', to gloss Karl Marx (in *The Eighteenth Brumaire of Louis Bonaparte*).

6. See the parallel discussion of the ethnographic present, indebted to Johannes Fabian, in the Introduction to the present collection. An important mid-sixteenth century source for such 'knowledge' is Hans Staden, a German mercenary seaman, whose remarkable adventures, including shipwreck and captivity by the Tupinamba Indians, were the basis of an immensely popular publishing venture in 1557. His book bore the ringing title *Truthful History and Description of a Landscape of Wild, Naked Cruel Man-Eating People in the New World of America*. Complete with woodcuts from his own vivid drawings which were later heavily adapted and plagiarised, this highly imaginative account proved to have great influence on subsequent visual and ethnographic representations of New World Indians. In his classic *History of Brazil* (1830) Robert Southey writes of Staden's sensational tale, 'it is a book of great value, and all subsequent accounts of the Tupi tribes rather repeat than add to the information which it contains'. Unconsciously, Southey is making precisely my point—reproduction of the 'already known' suffices to represent the Other. See Malcolm Letts (ed.), *Hans Staden: The True History of his Captivity, 1557* (London, 1928). For a critique of Staden on cannibalism see W. Arens, *The Man-Eating Myth* (New York, 1979), pp.22-30.

7. John Jones, *The Egotistical Sublime* (London, 1954), p.63; Mary Jacobus, *Tradition and Experiment in Wordsworth's Lyrical Ballads (1798)* (Oxford, 1976), pp.180-1.

8. See, for example, P.J. Keating, *The Working Classes in Victorian Fiction* (London, 1971), p.32ff and p.105 for metaphors equating the working class

with 'savages' and the novelist as 'explorer' in 'Darkest England'. Also Catherine Gallagher, *The Industrial Reformation of English Fiction* (Chicago, 1985), pp.3-35 on the worker/slave metaphor. Such metaphoric representations heavily determined Victorian ways of seeing.

9. H. Alan Cairns, *Prelude to Imperialism: British Reactions to Central African Society 1840-1890* (London, 1965), p.xii.

10. Philip Curtin, *The Image of Africa: British Ideas and Action 1780–1850* (Madison, WI, 1963), p.vi.

11. Important works on the representation of Africa in the latter part of the century include D. Hammond and A. Jablow, *The Africa That Never Was* (New York, 1970); B.V. Street, *The Savage in Literature* (London, 1975); William Schneider, *An Empire for the Masses: The French Popular Image of Africa, 1870-1900* (Westport, CT, 1982); M. McCarthy, *Dark Continent: Africa as seen by Americans* (London, 1983); H. Ridley, *Images of Imperial Rule* (London, 1983).

12. Quoted in Ruth Slade, *King Leopold's Congo* (Oxford, 1962), p.32.

13. Hammond and Jablow, *The Africa That Never Was*, p.96.

14. In the interests of brevity, this essay does not address the distinction which should theoretically be made between Conrad and Marlow. It is of course a central and complex issue for a critical understanding of the novel as a whole and for a fuller discussion see my *Heart of Darkness* (Milton Keynes, 1989).

15. Joseph Conrad, *Heart of Darkness* (Harmondsworth, 1980), pp.66, 68-9, 80. All further references will be taken from this Penguin edition and will be included within the text.

16. The *O.E.D.* definition, which first instances the word in 1851, cleverly hedges its bets: 'of, belonging to, or existing in the period antecedent to history, or to the first historical accounts of people'. That equivocation precisely marks the sliding between the prehistoric as something out of time (and therefore not sharing our history or nature) and something before the time for which we have records. (It is as if these 'primitive savages' exist only when we come along to write about them—which is a little like saying Livingstone 'discovered' Lake Victoria when, perhaps for reasons of resemblance, he named it after his queen, and so powerfully re-inscribed it in the map of European 'knowledge' of Africa.)

17. W. Arens, *The Man-Eating Myth*, argues that there is no serious anthropological evidence demonstrating widespread cannibalism. Although he may be overstating his case when he suggests it is *merely* mythical, he does show how confidently held was the European *belief* in its existence. What is pertinent here are the cultural uses to which the idea of cannibalism is put and how widespread was the 'need' for its existence.

RON TAMPLIN

Noblemen and Noble Savages

I want to look at three nineteenth-century accounts of travels in the Pacific, all comparatively little known, and all undertaken by members of the English upper classes. The lordliest of all is George Herbert, the Earl of Pembroke, who with Dr. George Henry Kingsley wrote an account of Tahiti and various of the Society Islands, Raritonga and Samoa, and finally, of shipwreck in the Fijian group.[1] Their book, *South Sea Bubbles* (1872) was thought by Louis Becke, among the liveliest of the Pacific's authors, to be one of 'the best and *truest* books of Polynesian life ever written'. (The others Becke mentions are Herman Melville's *Typee* and *Omoo*.)[2]

In 1878, Lady Brassey published *A Voyage in the Sunbeam*, an account of her *en famille* round-the-world voyage, 1876–1877.[3] In the main, I have confined myself to the sections on the Paumotus, Tahiti and Hawaii. My third and latest book is *Sunshine and Surf*, again jointly authored.[4] This is an account of Lord Albert Osborne's turn-of-the-century Pacific journey. It is written up, in fact, by his companion Douglas Hall, incorporating Lord Albert's 'valuable hints and suggestions', and takes in Tahiti and the Society Islands, the Marquesas, the Paumotus, New Zealand, Fiji, Samoa and Hawaii.[5]

I would not want to make any great claims for these books—certainly nothing in the way of Becke's commendation of *South Sea Bubbles*, which may well be logrolling. To turn to Robert Louis Stevenson's *In the South Seas* after a prolonged reading in Pembroke, Brassey and Hall is to glimpse a paradise beyond words. Still, they are all readable and have their moments. What emerges most strongly for me is the way our recognitions, and so our representations, are typed by our interests and our backgrounds. We see what we can see, and we can see what we want to see. Our evidences reveal ourselves. And in saying this I am not wishing to set up three pleasant enough English aristocrats. Let loose objective and cool social scientists, Viennese doctors, Parisian radicals,

thirty-two-toothed American fieldworkers, the best in the West on
anyone anywhere, and all will hold up mirrors to themselves and
distortedly read the features they see as clues to the ground of their own
being. And when the traffic is the other way, the Samoan at the
Sorbonne, the clues will be self-directed still. Nonetheless, if point of
view influences what people see, and so leads us to expect partiality in
their view, partiality may also be partial truth. In this particular case,
aristocrats may, by their peculiar position in their own society, have the
opportunity for special insight into Polynesian society. Not that we can
assume an aristocratic homogeneity; I suspect that Pembroke, Brassey
and Osborne would be a little chary of each other.

To begin with the question of opportunity. Undoubtedly money
and leisure allowed aristocrats a particular sort of uncommitted intervention into remote societies if they had the inclination to go to them.
I say 'uncommitted' because commitment either to career, to simple
existence or to faith would characterise French colonial civil servant,
New Bedford whaler, L.M.S. missionary alike, in a way which would
not touch the nonchalance of Albert Osborne's decision to visit the South
Seas, as an exotic change from the depths of his London club in winter
(p.1).

As to money, Francis Galton's qualifications for travel in *The Art of
Travel* catch just such an atmosphere of aristocratic availability. 'If you
have health, a great craving for adventure, at least a moderate fortune,
and can set your heart on a definite object, which old travellers do not
think impracticable, then—travel by all means'.[6] Uncommitted leisure
time and spare cash give the aristocrat a head start here. But there is
another spur, one which finds its clearest delineation in Rousseau, but
has in various guises much greater antiquity: that nobility resides in the
primitive as clearly as it does in heredity, and so the aristocrat is
implicitly encountering his *alter ego*. It is perhaps the supreme insouciance, and in its various ways constitutes the mind of Tony Benn
as it does the early yearnings for working-class associations documented
in Stephen Spender's *World Within World*, or indeed the documentary
fiction of George Orwell. Yeats' dream of the nobleman, beggar and the
saint is kindred. All these are men, except perhaps Orwell, who would
not be seen dead at a dogtrack. One of the clearest mythic accounts of
this conjunction is to be found in pastoral, with its tripartite in-
corporative view of society, the Town, the Court and the Country, but
the Gothic similarly recognises and incorporates emotions and psychological impulses, named primitive, into the libraries of sophistication.
In all these areas we incorporate into ourselves unrecognising ancestors,

and do with them what we will, with seigneurial rights. Consider Alexander Russell in his *Aristocrats of the South Seas*:

> The old South Seas was ruled by an aristocracy who were descended from the gods. They were tall, handsome and intelligent. They possessed a skin that was often but the palest of browns. The features of some were astonishingly like those of a European. They followed a rigid code of honour, went to 'college', were highly skilled in the art of debate and loved everything that was beautiful.
>
> The lower classes were intensely loyal to their divine masters. They fought fiercely for them and joined them without hesitation as they roamed the vast Pacific in their tiny ships.[7]

More mystical, less patronising, but related in its enforcement of a role upon Pacific peoples, is Frederick O'Brien, writing in 1919, in the face of the accelerating depopulation of the Pacific islands:

> Some day when deeper poverty falls on Asia or the fortunes of war give all the South Seas to the Samurai these islands will again be peopled. But never again will they know such beautiful children of nature, passionate and brave, as have been destroyed here. They shall have passed as did the old Greeks, but they will have left no written record save the feeble and misunderstanding observations of a few alien visitors.[8]

Add to all these Golden Ages, primitive Utopias, the Gothic frisson of the cannibal isles, and the South Seas can be everything that psychologies demand. Immediately, though, my concern is to present 'the feeble and misunderstanding observations' of my three (or five) alien visitors.

I have spoken of their lack of commitment in the missionary or the administrative sense. And indeed they more assume an imperial position than seek to extend it. There is nothing in any of them like, for example, the closing sentiments of Darwin's *Voyage of the Beagle*: 'It is impossible for an Englishman to behold these distant colonies without a high pride and satisfaction. To hoist the British flag, seems to draw with it, as a certain consequence, wealth, prosperity, and civilization'.[9] Nor do we find anything with the prophetic sweep of J.A. Froude's last words in *Oceana*:

> ... if, in short, we let it be seen that we have changed our nature, and are not the same men with those who once made our country feared and honoured, then, in ceasing to deserve respect, we shall cease to be respected. The colonies will not purposely desert us, but they will look each to itself, knowing that from us, and from their connection with us, there is nothing more to be hoped for. The cord will wear into a thread, and any accident will break it.[10]

Besides this, Lady Brassey is grocerly and so I suppose only prophesies, in the flesh, enterprise culture:

> I speak from personal experience when I say that every necessity of life on board ship, and many luxuries, can be procured at Tahiti. American tinned fruits and vegetables beat English ones hollow. Preserved milk is uncertain—sometimes better, sometimes worse, than what one buys at home. Tinned salmon is much better. Australian mutton, New Zealand beef, and South Sea pork, leave nothing to be desired in the way of preserved meat. Fresh beef, mutton and butter are hardly procurable, and the latter, when preserved, is uneatable. I can never understand why they don't take to potting and salting down for export the *best* butter, at some large Irish or Devonshire farm, instead of reserving that process for butter which is just on the turn and is already almost unfit to eat. (p.240)

But their commitment is to experience, seeking after what Paul Fussell calls 'venues of the palm tree'.[11] The islanders are naturally puzzled at this impulse. Lady Brassey describes the reactions of the inhabitants of Maitea:

> Most of the natives seemed puzzled to comprehend why we had visited the island at all. 'No sell brandy?'—'No.' 'No stealy men?'—'No.' 'No do what then?' Their knowledge of English was too limited to enable us to make them understand that we were only making a voyage of circumnavigation in a yacht. (p.217)

It is not merely that the islanders' English isn't too hot, not to mention the Brasseys' Paumotuan, but that purposeless voyaging is a sort of curiosity, perhaps quainter than all the 'quaint customs' our travellers observe. Where the islanders perceive a use, they are alert. Thus, on the same island:

> the natives seemed quite *au fait* in the matter of monetary transactions and exchanges. For an English sovereign they would give you change at the rate of five dollars. Chilian or United States dollars they accepted readily, but Brazilian currency they would not look at. (p.216)

Lady Brassey, true to the mercantilist origins of her money, is acute to and observant of trade:

> Mr. Godfroi gave us rather an amusing account of the manner in which their negotiations with the natives are conducted. The more civilised islanders have got beyond barter, and prefer hard cash in American dollars for their pearls, shells, cocoa-nuts, sandal-wood, &c. When they have received the money, they remain on deck for some time discussing their bargains among themselves. Then they

peep down through the open skylights into the cabin below, where the most attractive prints and the gaudiest articles of apparel are temptingly displayed, alongside a few bottles of rum and brandy and a supply of tobacco. It is not long before the bait is swallowed; down go the natives, the goods are sold, and the dollars have once more found their way back into the captain's hands. (pp.237-8)

The key words to define her attitude here are first, of course, 'amusing' and then 'The more civilised islanders have got beyond barter'. The presumption that a greater degree of civilisation brings with it a preference, however temporary, for American dollars, which can be used for 'the gaudiest articles of apparel', 'rum', 'brandy' and 'tobacco' is not one that J.A. Froude goes along with. In Hawaii his prophetic mode is again fuelled:

> I wandered about the environs looking at the people and their ways, and wondering at the nature of our Anglo-American character, which was spreading thus into all corners of the globe, and fashioning everything after its own likeness. The original, the natural, the picturesque, goes down before it as under the wand of a magician. In the place of them springs up the commonplace and the materially useful. Those who can adopt its worship and practice its liturgy, it will feed, and house, and lodge on the newest pattern, set them in a way of improving their condition by making money, of gaining useful knowledge, and enjoying themselves in tea-gardens and music-halls; while those who cannot or will not bend, it sweeps away as with the sword of the destroyer.[12]

What all nineteenth-century travellers encounter in the South Seas are societies whose terms are being changed, their integuments ripped apart. The travellers, of course, are among the instruments of change. And curiously enough the very haphazard and fortuitous, uncomplicated nature of their observations means that these travellers take for granted the existence of a community, take for granted the reality of culture contact. It would be too complicating to do other than that, and the account would not be written, the anecdote would not have a place without that first assumption or even concession. This is to say they may not know what makes Polynesian society tick but they know that it *is*. Their views have less value as ethnographic description but much at the pragmatic level of observing a society as it is. Because of this Lady Brassey's particular mercantilist interests are of value, since the ramifications of capital are a key agent of change. Thus her acute and fashion-conscious observation of the women on Bow Island suggests, but does not articulate, a number of possible understandings relating to change in dress, and cloths made in Europe and America specifically for 'native' trade, or at least for classes or races whom Lady Brassey did not normally meet.

> We saw three women, one very old, with nothing but a palm-leaf mat as a covering, the others dressed in the apparently universal costume, consisting of a long bright-coloured gown, put into a yoke at the shoulders, and flowing thence loosely to the ground, which completely conceals the wearer's form, even to the tips of her toes. I think these dresses must come from England or America, for they are evidently machine-made, and the cotton-stuff of which they are composed has the most extraordinary patterns printed on it I ever saw. Cherry and white, dark blue and yellow or white stripes, red with yellow spots, and blue with yellow crosses, appear to be the favourite designs. The women seemed gentle and kind, and were delighted with some beads, looking- glasses, and knives I gave them, in return for which they brought us quantities of beautiful shells. (pp.208-9)

There is a covert sense here of Lady Brassey not being implicated in other than innocent change in the word 'delighted'. This contrasts with the assumed degeneracy of the *resident* white man, whom she sees as an agent of malign change. This clearly involves an assumption about her own proprieties which I suspect are class-determined and maternalistic.

> The natives made us understand that on the other side of the entrance to the lagoon, in the better sort of house we had noticed, there resided a white man. He did not, however, make his appearance during our visit, and I imagine he must have been one of those individuals called 'beachcombers', referred to in so many of the books that treat of the South Sea Islands,—a sort of ne'er-do-well Englishman or American, rather afraid of meeting any of his own countrymen, but very clever at making a bargain between a ship's crew and the natives, with considerable profit to himself. (p.209)

There is an early evidence of this attitude and its consistency when, still in the English Channel, her children's Persian kitten 'Lily' is lost overboard. A heavy sea prompts them to put into Torbay, and at Torquay railway station the following incident occurred:

> Nothing more having been heard of our poor little kitten, we can only conclude that she has gone overboard. Just as we were leaving the railway-station, however, we saw a small white kitten with a blue ribbon round its neck; and all the children at once exclaimed, 'There's our Lily'! We made inquiries, and found that it belonged to the young woman at the refreshment-room, who, after some demur, allowed us to take it away with us, in compliance with Muriel's anxious wish, expressed on her face. (pp.2-3)

Now this annexation of a menial's pet to placate some spoilt children is the sort of *force-majeure* that her husband Tom exercises in an hotel in Hawaii:

> We went to eleven o'clock service at the cathedral. Later, Tom read the evening service to the men, and we afterwards landed and dined late at the hotel; so late, indeed, that we could hardly get anything to eat, and they began to shut up the room and put out the lights before we had half done. Luckily, we were a large party, and an indignant protest and threatened appeal to the landlord brought the Chinese waiters to their senses, and induced them to grant us half an hour's law. (p.282)

It is consistent with her view that 'sailors are more like children than grown-up men, and require as much looking after' (pp.192-3), and the maternal reproof hovering inadequately over incidents in Tahiti, regarding the behaviour of the crew.

My point here is that when she speaks of islanders, her views of them are attuned to the condescension she shows towards sailors and menials. It is never unkindly, but Polynesians are clearly placed. They live in idyllic surroundings. Tahiti is 'a fairy-like scene, to describe which is almost impossible, so bewildering is it in the brightness and variety of its colouring' (pp.220-1). And they live up to these surroundings, 'clad in the gayest robes and decked with flowers'. Fishing by torchlight on the reef off Papiete, 'the fine figures of the natives, lighted up by the flickering torches, and standing out in bold relief against the dark blue starlit sky, would have served as models for the sculptors of ancient Greece' (p.223). As models note, not the sculptors, a point which can be developed from distinctions she draws in Hawaii looking at portraits of generations of the Royal Family there, 'the early ones attired in their feather capes, the later ones dressed in European costumes. Most of them were the work of native artists, but the portraits of Kamehameha II and his queen were painted, during their visit to England, by a good artist' (pp.285-6). The word 'good' is key, for it contrasts directly with 'native'. In the museum in the new government buildings in Honolulu she sees:

> the old feather war cloaks, like the ancient *togas* of the Romans. They are made of thousands of yellow, red, and black feathers, of the *oo*, *mamo*, and *cine*, taken singly and fastened into a sort of network of string, so as to form a solid fabric, like the richest velvet or plush, that glitters like gold in the sunlight. The helmets, made of the same feathers, but worked on to a frame of perfect Grecian shape, similar to those seen in the oldest statuary or on the Elgin marbles, are even more artistic and elegant. Whence came the idea and design? Untutored savages could scarcely have evolved them

out of their own heads. Some element of civilisation, and of highly artistic civilisation too, must surely have existed among them at some remote period of their history. (p.277)

Just as Herrick's sense of England, as he muses in the Papiete calaboose in Stevenson's *The Ebb Tide*, incorporates into it the Roman Virgil, so Lady Brassey's sense of Europe easily assimilates Romans and Greeks into continuity with herself—representative of civilisation as she is—a continuity which seeks to dispossess contemporary Polynesians of their own cultural and aesthetic achievements. Her acquisitiveness is that of the curio collector, not the connoisseur. Neither standpoint has a great deal of virtue, in the end, but in the curio-seeker curiosity, not respect, predominates. Thus in the museum she sees specimens of 'all the ancient native weapons such as bows, arrows, swords, and spears', and remarks, 'now, alas! no longer procurable' (p.276). The use of weapons, of course, is another permitted skill. With bows and arrows the Hawaiians 'are as clever as all savages'; 'They are swift as deer, when they choose, though somewhat lazy and indolent' (p.270). Surfing similarly, while she recognises the skill of it, 'looked a most enjoyable amusement, and I should think that, to a powerful swimmer, with plenty of pluck, the feat is not difficult of accomplishment' (p.270).

Lady Brassey operates an odd sort of sleight of hand over the Hawaiian Royal Family, who after all had assimilated to themselves enough of the panoply of European Royalty to make it clear they are the real thing:

At three we were to go to the Royal Mausoleum. This was a special privilege, and, I believe, the greatest compliment that has been paid to us anywhere. No foreigners are allowed to enter, except admirals on the station; and very few inhabitants of Honolulu have ever seen the interior. The King has one key, the Dowager Queen Emma another, and the Minister of the Interior the third.

On our way up the hill to the Mausoleum, there was a funeral going on, very much after the style of an Irish wake, in one of the dwellings of the poorer class. The house was decorated with flags, and was crowded with people, all dressed in black, and generally with bright yellow *leis* over their heads and necks. They had evidently come from some distance, judging by the number of carts and wagons drawn up outside the door. Several people were sitting in an upper verandah. The corpse was laid out in the lower room, facing the road, as we could see through the open windows and door. It was surrounded by mourners, and four women were waving large *kahilis* slowly backwards and forwards in front of it. (pp.290-1)

No doubt had she witnessed a Royal funeral it too would have been 'very much after the style of an Irish wake', and had at least some kinship with a funeral 'in one of the dwellings of the poorer class'. But the magnificence of the Mausoleum and its generations of coffins mentally preserves Lady Brassey's hierarchical view of society.

There is finally an instance of the Brasseys being subjected to the same curiosity which they themselves had lavished on Oceanic artefacts as they assiduously collected 'heterogeneous cargo and multitudinous packages'. The Hawaiian King visits their yacht:

> His Majesty is a tall, fine-looking man, with pleasant manners, and speaks English perfectly and fluently. He and the Prince visited and examined every corner of the yacht and looked, I think, at almost every object on board. The pictures, curiosities, engines, and our various little contrivances for economising space, seemed to interest them the most. The inspection occupied at least an hour and a half; and when it was over, we had a long chat on deck on various subjects. The Prince of Wales's visit to India, and the Duke of Edinburgh's voyage round the world, were much discussed. I think the King would like to use them as a precedent, and see a little more of the world himself. His voyage to, and stay in America, he thoroughly enjoyed. (p.288)

Clearly, Lady Brassey sees His Majesty's interest as dictated by his recognition of a technological superiority in the yacht's design, which he would like to imitate. But earlier, when 'observing the native ways of living' at the halfway house on the way back from the volcanic crater of Kilauea, she:

> made an unsuccessful attempt to induce the woman of the house to part with her orange-coloured *lei*. I bought some *tappa* and mallets, however, with some of the markers used in colouring the cloth, and a few gourds and calabashes, forming part of the household furniture. (p.265)

By analogy with Lady Brassey's sense of the King's interest, no doubt the woman of the house could reasonably speculate whether her distinguished visitor was planning to furnish her house in England with calabashes and set up a tapa-cloth factory there, beating wonders out of English oak bark. But clearly there is curiosity and there is curiosity.

A couple of days earlier she had tried to buy this same *lei* from the woman but no inducement would persuade her to part with the necklace. 'It was the first she had ever made, and I was afterwards told that the natives are superstitiously careful to preserve the first specimen of their handiwork' (p.255-6), Lady Brassey writes, a little puzzled that cash cannot override custom.

The foregoing account may seem to be unduly heavy on Lady Brassey. It is not meant to be. She is for the most part sympathetic, largely caring, certainly brave, imaginative and genuinely interested in and observant of what she sees. All I wish to point out is that what she sees and what she is interested in are heavily conditioned. And what she does is to give credit to those things which reflect an affinity with her own interests. She can be enthusiastic about the South Seas where she perceives such an affinity. She never really understands a gift-giving culture, nor one with little concept of capital and cash crops, but its beauties and kindnesses easily assimilable to supposed European ideals make it difficult not to be comfortable there. Insofar as there is an 'other', it is something degraded from what she sees as the best of the present, either towards primitivism, as with the imported Kingsmill Islanders she meets in Tahiti, 'a wild savage-looking set, very inferior to the Tahitians in appearance' (p.231), or as it is corrupted by inferior European models. 'I think', she writes, 'if the many instances of the murder of ships' and boats' crews could be thoroughly sifted to the bottom, it would be found that most of them were acts of reprisal and revenge for brutal atrocities committed on the defenceless natives' (p.218). There is the preservative urge in her, that travel, as it moves towards tourism, promotes. Hence her distress that you can't get spears in Hawaii, not even for ready money. There is the mercantile urge which sees markets for Devon butter. And there is an acquisitive urge, which distorts local custom, both towards trade and towards an external and powerful domination, a demand enforcing supply. In her account we are prepared for it all in the refreshment room on Torquay station.

Sunshine and Surf starts unpromisingly enough, launching out with nothing particular to do from 'a cosy corner' of Osborne and Hall's London club. Indeed, if we are to judge by the preface, their impressions of 'the amusement they got out of the quaint manner and customs of the natives' won't be all that rewarding. But Osborne and Hall, anxious not to seem too serious, disinclined to produce 'a monument of scientific research', and, perhaps, to disarm judgement, are a bit self-deprecating. Their very laid-backness gives them a measure of purchase in the South Seas. They do not have the reformer's zeal but they can see good and bad. They are not acquisitive nor entrepreneurial but they are keen to see and to experience.

Often enough, they don't extrapolate from what they see and hear. On Atuana in the Marquesas, they write that the competitive dancers at the annual feast

> were, without exception, the best we saw in all our voyaging; and no wonder, considering that each village had been practising for weeks, this being their one excitement of the year. A gendarme told

me that the greatest punishment he could impose on a native—far
worse than ordinary fine or imprisonment—was to prevent him
going to these festivities; but after all, this is nothing extraordinary,
when one considers that they are only big, grown-up children.
(pp.142-3)

Now in this, there are a number of useful observations, about the social
centrality and importance of dancing and communal, competitive festi-
vity, and colonial recognition of this adjusted to a scale of punishment,
but the conclusion that the Marquesans are 'only big, grown-up
children' is swallowed whole from their evolutionary, Victorian times.
There is a touch of comedy in it, because Lord Albert and his companion
can be fairly childlike at times. They are delighted by the practical jokes
the crew and various passengers play on a chauvinistic Frenchman on
their voyage from San Francisco to Tahiti on the brigantine *Tropic Bird*:
Lady Brassey would certainly have seen them as rather like sailors,
mildly irresponsible in a waggish, aristocratic sense, of course—like the
permissions British society now gives to yuppies and university rugby
clubs, as opposed to football hooligans and lager louts.

At heart, Osborne and Hall are clubbable men and tend to see the
world as accommodation, more or less good, but never insupportable.
San Francisco had been particularly good and they arrived 'just in time
for the first draghunt under the auspices of the Burlingame Club; and
considering what a short time it is since they had started the game, they
had some very creditable mounts, and most of the people were turned
out very well' (p.4). They notice too that in the bars, the most popular
champagne is 'Mumm', the reason being 'when a "citizen" is three parts
intoxicated he may not be able to pronounce such difficult words
as, say, "Deutz and Gelderman" or "Perier Jouet- but even at his
last gasp is able to stutter out "Mumm" ' (p.7). It is with such a
background—how different from the home life of our dear Lady
Brassey— that our aristocrat and his acolyte launch themselves upon the
Pacific.

Their appraisals of the inhabitants are appreciative but distinctly
'horsey', at least as far as the men go. In the Marquesas, they respond
to 'the splendid physique of these islanders' (p.169), and at Papara on
Tahiti, they stay with Tati, son of a 'London Jew', and a daughter of
'the then reigning King Pomare (no connection with the champagne of
similar name)'. Osborne and Hall comment:

> As usual with the descendants of the white man and the daughters
> of the chiefs and kings of South Sea blood, their physique is
> extremely fine. Not only was our host himself a very fine specimen

of manhood, but he had three stalwart sons staying with him who
were also far above the European standard of manly beauty. (p.177)

As well as the air of the 'fancy' here there is too a sense of aristocrat
recognising aristocrat.

Osborne and Hall have a keen eye for the women. For instance, the
Samoans, 'especially the women, are without exception one of the
handsomest brown races in the world; a great many of the girls have
quite European features, and are well up to the standard of beauty in
Europe' (p.252). There is the sense here of sizing up the 'girls', somewhat
in the marketable sense, familiar from Thackeray or Trollope. It is the
eye of Europe, and responding to 'standards' made in Europe. Those
standards easily, not to say eagerly, accommodate to the Polynesian, but
not so easily to the Melanesian or the Negroid. In Samoa, Osborne and
Hall remark: 'The chief beauty of the native women is their lovely skin,
as soft as velvet, and their long, soft, glossy hair, with no trace of negro
fuzziness in it, and both of these they are very proud of' (p.266).

But even with the Melanesian Fijians, they can appreciate style,
suitably assimilated to the known:

> The Fijian, although now one of the most civilised of South Sea
> Islanders, has a most savage aspect. . . . and, of course, as every one
> knows, their great shock head of hair sticking straight on end, and
> bleached a light yellow with lime, is most impressive. Some of the
> girls had bleached their hair to quite a fashionable peroxide tint,
> which would have been the admiration of a chorus girl. (pp.207-8)

Whether it is a lack of knowledge or a greater reticence is not clear, but
Lady Brassey seemed to know the Pacific islanders less closely than
Osborne and Hall. 'Mother Grundy', they tell us in the section on Tahiti,
'would be rather shocked at some of the antics played at these bathing
parties, as the natives have not much sense of decency, according to
European ideas' (p.60), and the Samoans are 'for South Sea Islanders,
fairly moral in their own particular way' (p.252). Again they can
particularise the various communities. Speaking of a dance in Fiji, they
write,

> This was a true exhibition of skill in dancing and spectacular effect,
> and not, as is sometimes the case in the French islands, the prelude
> and excuse for a night of orgy. Such a thing as white officials having
> anything to do with native women is absolutely unknown in these
> islands; the man who did such a thing, or was even suspected of it,
> would be rigorously tabooed—a very different state of affairs to what
> exists, as I said before, in Tahiti. (p.222)

Nonetheless they too can dwell on the romantic image the islands

present. Describing bonita hunting at night on the reef in Tahiti—
'first-rate sport'—they write that 'the scene on the reef, with the great
waves roaring beside you, and the half-naked semi-savages lit up by the
glare of the torches, has a weird and picturesque beauty of its own'
(p.69). And at Atuana in the Marquesas: 'The girls are simple children
of Nature, and used to go into the water in Eve's costume before the
Fall, and very picturesque they used to look, just like bronze statues
come to life' (p.147).

Between them these descriptions indicate a dreamlike mixture of the
romantic, the paradisal, the classic, the Gothic and the primitive fit to
regale jaded clubland sensibilities. The Gothic frisson, just glimpsed in
the bonita hunt, is more fully presented in the Marquesas:

> One has to be careful in one's hospitality to the men. They are all
> arrant cannibals and savages at heart. Many of them had themselves
> tasted 'long pig' *i.e.* human flesh, and they had but the thinnest
> veneer of civilisation over them, which rubbed off at once when the
> liquor was in them. Then they had no fear of the white man, and
> one held one's life in one's hand. (pp.150-1)

Comically enough, when they do in fact meet in Fiji a substantial link
with this Pacific cannibal past, at Bau, 'the old cannibal stronghold of
the kings of Fiji', and now a centre for the Wesleyan missionaries, the
incident has an Evelyn Waugh-like quality about it:

> Next morning Thakambau sent word that he would like to show us
> round his domain; so off we started, and very interesting it was,
> although, as far as I can remember, the chief thing he pointed out
> to us was the old cannibal high place, situated in the centre of the
> village, surrounded by a high fence, inside which were some huge
> stones, where, old Thakambau told us, with an ugly gleam in his
> eye, he had often as a boy seen native and white men's heads dashed
> in before they were put in the ovens and cooked; and I must say,
> from the look in his eye, I should have been surprised if he would
> have strongly objected doing the same to us. (pp.213-4)

Thakambau then invites them to head a subscription list for a new
football club, which they do, commenting however, 'it is our strong
impression that they never have played and never will play football at
Bau' (p.214). There is a nice air of having been outwitted, precisely by
the very European means of the confidence trick, and it is refreshing.
It is recognition which is self-recognition. There is a similar scene in
Jack London's story, 'The Whale Tooth'. The zealous missionary, John
Starhurst, describes the Biblical creation of the world to the Fijian
high-chief, Mogondro, whose response is both shrewd and restrained:

'It is a story to frighten children with; but no man can believe it'.
'I am a man', the missionary said.
'True, you are a man. But it is not given to my dark understanding
to know what you believe'.
'I tell you, I do believe that everything was made in six days'.
'So you say, so you say', the old cannibal murmured soothingly.

In this passage London is imputing to Mogondro rationality and a degree
of irony in the face of the missionary's irrational credulity. It is a reversal
of the normal Western picture, and one in which London recognises his
own values in Mogondro.

Both London and Osborne and Hall are writing of a society in
transition, subject to the enormous pressures of Western contact. The
islanders in Fatuhiva in the Marquesas have an entrepreneurial response
to Osborne and Hall, that is as incongruous, if we live by stereotypes,
as Thakambau's football club subscription list.

The natives, who had learned from a roving trader that we were
coming, had collected all sorts of curios, which they brought round
in their canoes. Even in this far-off spot of the globe we discovered
that the art of making and faking-up curios was not unknown,
although their attempts at this latter process were so crude that they
would not have deceived even some of our recent millionaires. All
the same, we obtained one or two very unique specimens of stone
gods; but the bulk of the curios on this island had been long ago
collected by missionaries and others, and also a good many had been
sent to Paris for the previous Paris Exhibition, having been collected
by the gendarmes under orders from the Government. The Ger-
mans, by the way, seem to be the most industrious collectors, at
present, of South Sea curios. Several professors have been out to
these islands with, apparently, *carte-blanche* to purchase anything
they liked, at any price. (pp.167-8)

However nonchalant Osborne and Hall's tone, they are attentive observers. And their anecdotes remind us that we cannot 'represent' people
without representing 'society' and movement in that society. This is
because the anecdote depends upon exchange. Portraiture tends to cast
people as icons, in unchanging roles and hence as stereotypes. In the
case of Osborne and Hall, their anecdotes, centred as they are on the
meeting of cultures, suggest that peoples change as they meet the agents
of change, and that such change is not simply enforced from outside,
but also sifted, accepted and rejected from the inside. What they
construct and perceive in the Pacific is a mirror of their own receptivity
and, indeed, nonchalance. At Akoui, in the Marquesas, they meet the
prince consort, 'an engaging young Kanaka, about twenty-four years

old, who received us on the beach with that entire absence of ceremony which is one of the great charms of all South Sea Islanders' (pp.112-3). This 'entire absence of ceremony', of European starch, is the pulse behind their own anecdotal goodwill.

This is not, however, to be mistaken for insouciance. They are extremely critical, for example, of American policy and intrigue in Hawaii, leading to annexation. They are outspoken about British policy in Fiji, the islands being 'little better than a British slave colony' (p.223), and of the Governor, 'a man with very strong ideas, which are not always successful', a man with an 'autocratic thumb' (p.225ff). When Osborne and Hall visited, the Governor in question was Sir George O'Brien.

> He seemed much surprised when we said we wanted to explore the islands, and see as much of native life as we could. He did not appear to have done much of this sort of thing himself, and seemed to think we must be both rather cracked to want to do it. However, he kindly gave us a letter to the Colonial Secretary, telling him to give us every assistance in his power, and then, after cordially asking us to dine with him whenever we returned to civilisation, *i.e.* to Suva, bade us farewell for the present. He has rather a nice Government house, although it seems to have a superfluous amount of gables to it; the grounds are very extensive, and have attached to them a long private pier out into the lagoon, which is, however, very seldom used. (p.205)

The tone here, indirect as it is, becomes clear in its shading later when a letter to the *Fiji Times* about the use of forced labour to build Nabumakita Hospital is quoted. It ends, 'Sir George O'Brien never leaves his house, I understand, and so he has probably never heard anything about this matter' (p.227). They recognise too that in the present state of things, with Fiji as a Crown Colony, there is very little to be done, since power is at Westminster and 'any Members who spoke or asked questions about Fiji would get as their sole reward a caricature of themselves in *Punch*, dressed as a half-naked Fijian, with a club in his hand, dancing a war-dance—so little do people in England care or know of this far-off colony' (p.229).

Indentured labour on the cane plantations 'looks very like legalised slavery'. (p.220) In 'the blackbirding trade . . . a good many of the [Solomon] Islanders get accidentally killed under the humane persuasion of the recruiters when engaging labour' (p.258). Interestingly for a pair of travellers who can direct a quiet degree of irony at cant, they generally speak well of the missionaries, from the Mormons, who 'have a hard fight against all manner of misrepresentation' (p.64), through the Methodists, who 'appeared a fairly intelligent class of men' (p.208), to the Catholics, who seemed 'kindly, simple people really anxious to improve the condition of the natives, and not always trying to be the biggest bosses in the place' (p.231).

This willingness to see quite distinct points of view, each from its own centre, is a mark of Osborne and Hall's degree of recognition of things in their own terms. Thus a Fijian village presents huts, 'the finest specimens of savage architecture existing', the interiors 'elaborately decorated', sennit wound around the beams 'in beautiful arabesque designs', tapa cloth 'painted in bold, artistic patterns' (pp.214-5). Although they have no real sense of the significance of dancing in Polynesian culture, they at least perceive it is not merely entertainment. In Atuana in the Marquesas, the 'annual feast is really a most excellent idea. It not only keeps the natives in good temper, but it perpetuates and prevents being forgotten the old dances and songs of their nation, which, I am sorry to say, are fast dying out in other islands where they have no such annual gathering' (p.140).

And the Solomon Islanders 'are the most beautiful carvers imaginable; some of their canoes and other pieces of work are really works of art' (p.258). But it seems such a range of appreciations still must have its limits, some 'other'. The Solomon Islanders reveal it: 'They have most repulsive-looking faces compared to Samoans, and to the casual observer might very well have come from parts of Central Africa' (p.258). And in the villages of Northern Savaii in the Samoas, the same thought occurs. The natives are 'always cheerful, bright and hospitable', their customs 'interesting and often unique': 'The whole life here is so absolutely different to anything else in Europe, down to every detail, and yet it is not the savage, dirty, beastly life of many African villages'. Again a self-recognition within difference is at work here: 'These Polynesian Islanders are much further removed from niggers than they are from white men—a beautiful handsome race, with most cleanly habits' (p.282).

Although the earliest of the three books, I have left *South Sea Bubbles* to last. It is a more ambitious production than the grocerly *A Voyage in the Sunbeam* or the clubbable *Sunshine and Surf*. Its prefatorial sense of itself is that it includes 'the highest subjects', 'the most solemn philosophies', and although it disavows any ability for 'glorious master-pieces of word painting', there is a definite attempt at them:

> I can never forget the scene that burst upon my astonished and half-opened eyes as I turned out of bed one morning and found myself entering the port of Papiete. Great mountains, of every shade of blue, pink, grey, and purple, torn and broken into every

conceivable fantastic shape, with deep, dark mysterious gorges, showing almost black by contrast with the surrounding brightness. . . . And the natives! How well they match the scene! The women, with their voluptuous figures,—their unique, free, graceful walk,— their nightgowns . . . floating loosely about in a cool refreshing manner,—their luxuriant black tresses, crowned with a gracefully plaited Araroot chaplet, and further ornamented by a great flowing bunch of white 'Reva-Reva',—their delicious perfume of cocoa-nut oil (it is worth going to Tahiti for the smell alone),—and, above all, their smiling handsome faces, and singing, bubbling voices, full of soft cadences,—all this set off by the broken, scattered rays of green light shining through the shady avenues. Oh, that I were the artist that could paint it! (pp.10-11)

'Society Islandism' is seen as 'aimless pointless dreaminess', 'a kind of early Christian brotherly love coming over you, a delicious indolence, a refined gentleness of manner, and a blunting of the edge of your moral ideas' (p.14). And this is the prose style to go with it, 'utterly dreary to an incident-and-information-loving European reader' (p.14). The Earl and the Doctor assert the virtues of their 'brown friends', 'their natural unsophisticated impulse towards kindness, affection, and unselfishness, shortlived though it may be' (pp.18-9), against the mealy-mouthed standards of England. They meet bronze statues illumined by the blazing light of the torches on the reef, just as Lady Brassey and Osborne and Hall will, later in the century. They have a good, even learned, ear for the music. The tunes of European origin, but 'nativised',

> had a character of their own utterly unlike and far finer than Arabic, Turkish or any savage melody I ever heard. . . . extraordinary perfect time . . . and the strange metallic ring of every voice which . . . had a wild and curious effect, that was in perfect keeping with the savage grandeur of the whole scene. (pp.23-4)

They are also more attentive than Lady Brassey and Osborne and Hall to vegetation, birds and fish, and much of the description, while lavish, is valuable. In some matters they present more or less the same attitudes as one or other of the later travellers do. They are as confused by gift-giving as Lady Brassey, offering money in exchange in the English manner, but eventually do come to some sense of its importance. In Raritonga they remark, 'it really seems as if these people could not help giving' (p.196), and later in Samoa, they extend the discussion, when confronted by mild begging:

> Asking for tobacco seems here to mean little more than a form of kindly greeting. . . . Amongst many of these peoples, not only is begging or asking for a thing unknown, but they have no word to

express thanks or gratitude. If they want a thing (amongst themselves) they take it, expecting their neighbours to do the same by them. There are no thanks, because it is a right, not an obligation, and there is nothing to be thankful for. (p.217)

They are as prone as Osborne and Hall to perceiving people as specimens. On Bora-Bora, the women 'are fine great animals' (p.131) and in Samoa,

> the sulu in which the men were dressed permitted us to see their glorious forms in full perfection, and there are few finer races in the world than these Samoans,—a little heavy and provincial perhaps . . . but still magnificent men. . . . Time was when I used to think that no sculptor of the 'nude' could ever be worth his salt, unless he had spent a year or two in Africa. Now, I should most certainly send him to the Society Islands, where he will see his fellow-men as they ought to be. . . . (pp.221-2)

But Dr. Kingsley adds a medical edge to the values of the sculptor and the connoisseurs of the flesh:

> The roundness and development of the upper part of the back and arms [of a Society Islander], from constant use of the spear, is most beautiful; and when not disfigured by elephantiasis, which is too often the case, the lower leg and ankle are perfect; as superior to the coarse limbs of a Maori as the fetlock of a thoroughbred is to that of a cart-horse. (pp.68-9)

The Earl and the Doctor relish the relaxedness of Polynesian culture as much as Osborne and Hall will do later, but record it as it seems to work within society and not just as unaffected courtesy towards themselves. The 'tone of perfect equality in social life' between the Royal family in the Society Islands and their subjects seems 'essentially unbarbaric' characterised by 'unsnobbishness', yet 'all have the greatest respect for high birth, or rather, good ancestry'.

There are a number of points where they stress the superiority of Pacific ways over the European or English: 'To compare the "Broom-road" of Huahine with the streets of an English town after nightfall, would be a most infamous libel on the former', they say. 'What immorality there may be, is infinitely less immoral in Huahine than in England, as one might easily prove did one care to go into the foul subject' (p.97). And when a white man gone native on Taha refuses to speak ill of King Tamatoa, 'an awful scoundrel', they comment: 'So politics were barred. How unlike the glorious freedom of my own country, where any foul-mouthed rascal, with the gift of the gab, may get up and abuse Her Majesty in public with impunity' (p.109).

The Earl and the Doctor tend rather to share this political discretion. Thus over the labour ships and blackbirding, among other pros and cons, this view is offered: 'Still I think that this shifting the inhabitants of these islands from one to another is a good thing if properly done, and is in fact the *only* way of civilising some of the more savage tribes' (p.156). And they quote a case in which a planter transporting native labour and whose ship is seized by a British man-of-war, wins his case in Sydney but is impoverished by the incident and loses both his ship and its human cargo. The reader is asked to remember that:

> the victim here was no long-shore loafer, no square-gin-drinking 'beach-comber', but a man of birth and education; and who would, in all possibility, have made his fortune had he not had the luck to win a lawsuit against a philo-negro captain of the navy. (pp.159-60)

The authors are arguing, reasonably enough, for effective regulation of the trade, but it is hard to think that they are not a bit too nonchalant about the nature of the trade itself.

In fact the language here which contrasts the 'long-shore loafer', 'square-gin-drinking beach-comber' with 'a man of birth and education' and coins the word 'philo-negro' (a lordly version of 'niggerlover') is beginning to reveal a set of prejudices and predispositions which are sufficiently masked when what is seen is simply a succession of pretty girls and magnificent men. But the effusions spent upon them are only an overload of interpretation which the authors import into the Pacific. Essentially, they do not represent the Pacific so much as use it as a counter in a range of predetermined arguments. The effusions are debased Rousseauism, innocent enough, but the more emphatic inter- pretations are driven by a facile progressivism, which everywhere substitutes speculation of the most generalised kind for observation. It is the rhetoric of Gibbon and Macaulay without the research. For example, the missionaries are an important and controversial instrument for change in the nineteenth-century Pacific. The Earl and the Doctor meet a number of missionaries whom they are deeply impressed by. They do not record visiting any Methodists or Roman Catholics. The final chapter of *South Sea Bubbles* is called 'The Missionaries' and is a wholesale and largely hearsay condemnation of virtually all Pacific missionary activity, but particularly of Methodists and Catholics, who seem to be concerned only with power, duplicity and money. The missionaries they do meet are Congregationalists of the London Mis- sionary Society. Pembroke writes of them:

> they struck me as being wonderfully good, intelligent, liberal,

practical men; not wilfully blinding their eyes to any imperfection in the success of their labours, or fanatically trying to force the natives all at once into their own groove, but patiently trying to make them peaceful and happy, and to instil into their minds a sense of the nobility and beauty of Christian morality, rather than any abstract and disputed dogmas. (p.299)

It is this switchback between eulogy and caricature which makes *South Sea Bubbles* a suspect book, its speculative heart and driven judgements, extraneous to the Pacific, not squaring with its observations.

The same holds true for its view of the Pacific peoples. Everywhere they give delight, but speculation renders them as splendid fossils fit only to be superseded. Man may be 'but an imperfectly developed animal: rising higher and higher as the ages roll on, with more perfectly developed organs permitting the freer action of a nobler soul.' . . . (p.201) and:

New or old, it is worth while to look at the coloured races of mankind as an instructive collection of fossils, which may be studied by the ethnologist as the others are by the geologist. There are some very old fossils of this sort to be found, like the habit of crouching . . . which . . . savours of the remembrance of tails; or the apey toes; . . .; the sharkey grin, no real smile, lighting up the face from within, but the mere removal of the lips from the hideously large and regular teeth; or the brown opaque eye, bloodshotten like that of a vicious horse, reminding one of a plover's egg with a boiled prune for a yolk, infinitely inferior in expression to that of a well educated dog. These are the sort of things I should call human fossils, and let us hope that they will be well-studied before they disappear. . . . (pp.201-2)

This, needless to say, is dangerous stuff. 'The coloured peoples' are given validity not by any inherent and self-possessed dignity but rather insofar as they are seen as providing evidence for our own self-image, filling in historical detail of how we got to where we are. It is no great concession that:

the pleasantest forms of the human fossil we have ever met with have been in the South Seas. India and the East are doubtless highly fossiliferous, and pleasantly so; but the great mass of specimens have been terribly worn, and have lost their real old edging and sharpness by civilisation. In the South Seas, in spite of the missionary, pure unpolished specimens may still be found. (p.203)

Indeed this passage betrays one of the corollaries of the tendency to see people as bearing a particular importance insofar as they act as indicators for our own self-image or stabilise some part of us that we find difficult

79

to come to terms with, 'the primitive' and so on. The corollary is that we do not wish them to change but to remain 'primitive', eternally representing something for us.

Pembroke's faults are really the faults of an educated and self-confident class, who know they know, but do not know what they do not know. Any evidence or sight is invariably fitted up into an all-embracing theory, whether of race, religion or custom. Thus while he is more acute to some of the ranges of meaning in Polynesian dance, he certainly lifts his eyes from the object in the following tour-de-force, this in Samoa:

> It would hardly do to describe the dancing very particularly; it was certainly pretty in its way, and of that style which I think Mr. Murray mentions in his *Handbook for Spain*, as having obtained amongst the 'improba Gaditana' which I supposed may be translated 'the improper Cadiziennes'. It is the same dance all over the world; from the gypsies of Grenada to the gawazee of Egypt; from the gawazee of Egypt to the nautch-girls of India; from the nautch-girls of India, all musk and patchouli, and silks and gems, to the dirty little gin, of Western Australia with her stinking bundle of possum skins, it is all the same; nay, even in the jig of Ireland and the almost pious reel of Scotland, Smell-fungus can detect the lingering relics of pagan impropriety. (pp.234-5)

The same sweep occurs in the treatment of religion—'from the storm-dropped stone at Huahine you get the gilded dome of St. Paul's' (p.88) is a characteristic leap, or from 'Maori Tohunga to the presbyterian minister' (p.122). The point of this rhetorical device is not simply to establish a continuity, which may or may not be valid, but to condemn each by association with the other. Thus the idea of sacrifice is presented not simply as a theological idea, arrived at within a variety of religions, and taking a variety of forms, but as a 'creation of the priestly mind' that has 'extended, through all ages' and, as such, constituting a corrupt creation (p.122). This travel through religions is occasioned by walking to an island marae in Raiatea and imaginatively reconstructing its past—'What horrible stories these stones could tell if they could speak!' (p.122). The Earl and the Doctor see what they want to see just as much as Lady Brassey, and Osborne and Hall. But they are far more dangerous because they lay greater claims for their conclusions.

Their views of the Pacific are, as with all these travellers, effusive and delighted, but there is a limit to their capacity for delight. On Bora-Bora, the Doctor writes:

> Heigh, ho! this is the last day in Paradise. After tomorrow we

shall see nothing but ugly copper-coloured savages, or dirty-black Fegeans; and then we shall return to sordid, practical, white people, black coals, shirt collars, actions for breach, and all that, growls the disconsolate P. (p.141)

And on Raritonga, the islanders: 'are still very charming, but their mouths and noses are altering. The face generally is growing coarser, and one begins to sniff the negro taint from far-distant Papua' (p.163).

There are other limitations on their goodwill too, notably the Maoris in New Zealand:

The Maori, moreover, in spite of his Christianity, seems to possess all the vices of both the western and eastern Polynesians without any of their virtues, except their bravery. He is as idle, immoral, and useless as a Tahitian, without his perfect manners, unselfish generosity and general kindliness. As snobbish, untruthful and avaricious as a Tongan, without his constructive and inventive power, he is a savage to the backbone, liking fighting better than any other occupation, and living a much better life when he is fighting than at any other time. (pp.313-4)

Clearly, even among Polynesians there are limits then, and Pembroke, with a balanced syntax which lends itself to false definition and studied oppositions, establishes clearly enough where they are for him.

Insofar as I wish to draw general conclusions from these specific nineteenth-century accounts of Polynesians, some of them, at least, must be methodological. Representation cannot be abstracted from a set of attitudes more widely observable in the person whose views we are assessing. Such views may be attributable to causes far away from the conditions of the people represented. They may derive from our social standing in our own society, from education or from habits ingrained there. They may even be pathological. But, in questions of culture contact, those views will be located in a coherent frame which has already operated elsewhere, if not always as extremely.

Representation is at its most useful when it does not seek the stationary, the monumental view. It is best seeing movement and hinting at reciprocity. We are speaking, that is, of cultural exchange, however unbalanced. This is why I prefer the anecdote to the portrait. Anecdote records movement. A society observed from outside is already a society in change. Portraits attempt to fix, often, sadly, to memorialise as an act of nostalgia. It may follow from this that the more apparently naive the observer, the more valuable the observations. They may be the least fixed and presumptuous of people, not because they cannot make formulations but because they have not succumbed to the formulations they might make. It certainly does follow that where we are predisposed (i.e. conditioned) to like some class or, in the case of these travellers, some people, we will attribute to them, or draw from within their range, those things which we like or applaud in ourselves. We recognise ourselves. It is also the case that, at least partially, we recognise others. When we do not see elements of ourselves, or refuse to countenance elements that we know and suspect in ourselves, then we recognise, or, more truly, create 'the other'. 'The others' may not be Sartre's 'hell', but they will be scapegoats; in these narratives, typically, Negroes, white trash, sometimes missionaries. As Frantz Fanon says, 'It is the racist who creates his inferior'.[13]

To sum up, then. Lady Brassey's mercantilism, condescension, maternalism are attitudes born in economic and class structures in England and cause her to project Polynesians in terms of their reactions to money transactions, as beautiful children, and to regret all change that is not seen as 'civilising'. Osborne and Hall are clubbable, benign, know they are fated not to be taken seriously, and so see a great deal, in a world which could be quite a well-run club, with a pleasant, if exotic, membership. The Earl and the Doctor have nearly all the answers, prepared on the lecture pads of England, in the new-minted evolutionary world. The Polynesians are pleasing fossils and to be observed as such, along with other interesting evidences, flora, fauna, vestigial behaviours, objects in a world understood as a world of objects. In all three narratives, the Polynesians too—quick on the uptake, clubbable or interesting phenomena though they may be—are yet a collective *alter ego*, charming to the travellers, a benign 'other', holding out possibilities beyond the country house, the engineering workshop, 'society', the club and the committee room. The scapegoat 'other' necessary to underpin this world arranged around their own predilections, to absorb to itself all that nightmares are made of, is always out of the picture: missionaries they never meet, beachcombers who avoid Europeans, but especially, preeminently, the Negro, away, hinted at on the Western Pacific rim, deep too, in the recesses of the mind, but in a figmented Africa, truly 'other'.

NOTES

1. The Earl and The Doctor [George Robert Charles Herbert and George Henry Kingsley], *South Sea Bubbles* (London, 1872). My page references,

which appear in the text, are to the Tauchnitz edition (vol. 1426) published in Leipzig in 1874.

2. Ed. T. Fisher Unwin, *Good Reading About Many Books Mostly By Their Authors* (Second Year) (London, 1895-6), p.289. Pembroke wrote the introduction for Becke's first book, *By Reef and Palm* (London, 1894).

3. Lady Annie Brassey, *A Voyage in the Sunbeam, Our Home on the Ocean for Eleven Months* (London, 1878). I have used the second edition, 1886, and page references appear in the text. There is a modern reprint with a useful introduction by George Millar, in the Century Seafarers series (London, 1984).

4. Douglas B. Hall and Lord Albert Osborne, *Sunshine and Surf, A Year's Wanderings in the South Seas* (London, 1901).

5. Hall and Osborne, preface, unnumbered. Other references appear in the text.

6. Francis Galton, *The Art of Travel; or, Shifts and Contrivances Available in Wild Countries* (1855); I quote from the 5th ed. (London, 1872).

7. Alexander Russell, *Aristocrats of the South Seas* (London, 1911), p.7.

8. Frederick O'Brien, *White Shadows in the South Seas* (London, 1919), p.450. For views of Pacific depopulation in the period, see Stephen H. Roberts, *Population Problems of the Pacific* (London, 1927).

9. Charles Darwin, *Journal of Researches into the Natural History and Geology of the Countries Visited during the Voyage of H.M.S. 'Beagle' Round the World*; I quote from the corrected and enlarged edition of 1845 (London: Ward, Lock and Co., 1890), p.368.

10. J.A. Froude, *Oceana, or England and her Colonies* (London, 1886), p.341.

11. Paul Fussell, *Abroad: British Literary Travelling Between the Wars* (Oxford, 1980), p.5.

12. Froude, *Oceana*, p.302.

13. Frantz Fanon, *Black Skin, White Masks* (1952). English translation by Charles Lam Markmann, 1967; I quote from the Paladin edition (London, 1970), p.65.

PETER QUARTERMAINE

Johannes Lindt: Photographer of Australia and New Guinea

An Australian historian recently observed that 'national identities are invented within a framework of modern Western ideas about science, nature, race, society, nationality'.[1] It is therefore anything but surprising that some 150 years of critical debate on the nature—or very existence—of 'Australian art' should involve discussion of such related topics. Debates on art and national identity often reveal more about the participants than about artists or their work: after all, the very idea of a national canon is itself largely a construct of an educational system which needs such a body of works in order to justify, and to perpetuate, its own existence and authority.[2] It is within such constraints that academic 'objectivity' operates, and so it is helpful to trace the influence of certain images of nationality, and to understand whose ends they serve. These questions are as central to Australian art as to Australian history or politics.[3]

Seen from overseas, 'Australian art' has usually meant painting, perhaps even certain periods, painters or paintings; since the appearance of such artistically self-conscious productions as *Picnic at Hanging Rock* (d. Peter Weir, 1975), not to mention the very different appeal of the *Mad Max* series, it may also mean film. However, it is less likely today than at the time of the Australian Centennial celebrations of 1888 that 'Australian art' will include photographic images. No photograph features in those visual images through which the nation defines itself—whether to itself, or to others—and which thereby contribute to its mythology.[4]

Invaluable as 'illustrations' or as source material, photographs are less frequently considered works of art; art is deemed 'imaginative', whereas photography is thought merely to record 'facts'. To adduce the influence of art on photography is informative; to suggest photographic influences

1. Simcoe Memorial, Exeter Cathedral, by John Flaxman, 1815.

2. Townshend Memorial, Westminster Abbey, by Robert Adam, 1761.

3. Drawing by Flaxman in preparation for the Simcoe Memorial.

4. 'The Commander in
Chief of the Cherokees', c.
1762, anonymous engraving.

5. Portrait of Joseph Brant, by George
Romney, 1775-76, now in the National
Gallery of Canada.

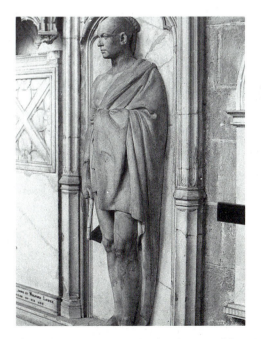

6. Native American figure in the Simcoe Memorial.

7. Woodcut of Tupinamba Indians, probably by Johann Froschauer, 1505.

8. 'English Church and Parsonage, Glenn Innis',
photograph by Johannes Lindt, n.d.

9. Untitled photograph by Johannes Lindt from
Aboriginal Natives from Clarence River District, 1875.

10. Untitled photograph by Johannes Lindt from
Aboriginal Natives from Clarence River District, 1875.

11. 'Camped', photograph by Johannes Lindt, n.d.

12. 'Near the Camp, Laloki River', photograph by
Johannes Lindt, 1885.

13. 'Motu Water Carrier—Port Moresby', photograph by
Johannes Lindt, 1885.

14. 'Native Teachers', photograph by Johannes Lindt, 1885.

15. 'Oasis in the Badlands', photogravure from a photograph by Edward S. Curtis, 1904.

17. 'Before the White Man Came—Palm Cañon', photogravure from a photograph by Edward S. Curtis, 1924.

16. 'Mosa—Mohave', photogravure from a photograph by Edward S. Curtis, 1903.

18. 'The Spirit of the Past—Apsaroke', photogravure
from a photograph by Edward S. Curtis, 1906.

on art is downright subversive, in that it seeks to 'reduce' art to the level of photography. Such attitudes not only still obscure photography's historical role in Australian art, but also prevent recognition of the medium's continuing importance. In examining the work of a successful and well known nineteenth-century photographer in Australia, Johannes Lindt (1845–1926), this essay seeks to clarify issues not only of visual coding, but also of national mythology; it argues that Lindt's most neglected photographs—those of New Guinea—are among his most important.[5] His photographs of native peoples question easy definitions of 'Australian art', and also alert us to the significance of conventions of perception and depiction in the visual arts.

When in the 1870s Lindt chose to style himself 'artist photographer', the respective roles of painting and photography had been contested worldwide for over three decades; often cast as inimical to art ('foe-to-graphic' as magazine cartoons put it), photographers for their part frequently sought the status of painting. In fact the two media traded influences freely, though rarely openly, from the start. Contemporary debate on photography's social role and status bears upon Lindt's work since much of this depicted the native peoples of Australia and New Guinea, themselves irrelevant to Australian mythology because perceived as devoid of all status and power: the embarrassing Aboriginal presence was accommodated by the belief that these people were doomed to extinction, while New Guinea's inhabitants could be regarded as exotically interesting because reassuringly distant. These peoples were photographed as 'other': the white settler population was interested in learning *about* them, a quasi-scientific attitude which presupposed a controlling position. The photographic images produced by Australian photographers sold to a metropolitan and international consumer market. Such prints doubly privileged the purchasers since, although reflecting their own aesthetic (natives clothed, and posed with decorative artefacts) they also supposedly granted direct access to the culture depicted; their use as raw evidence by anthropologists and ethnographers certainly assumed this.[6]

One reassuring piece of information communicated by images thus framed was that their subjects formed no part of that 'progress' represented by the metropolitan viewer (and, indeed, by the technology of photography itself). Photography is here no mere handmaid of empire, but a shaping dimension of it: formal imperial power structures institutionalised the attitudes and assumptions necessarily entailed in viewing another individual as a subject for photography. Such assumptions die hard, and as late as 1982 the Introduction to the extensive exhibition, the *History of the Commonwealth in Photographs,* displayed at the Brisbane Commonwealth Games that year, could accept rather than question attitudes somewhat reminiscent of nineteenth-century imperialism: 'As new territories came under European control and administration, and were opened up for settlement, it became standard practice for the enterprising photographer to document both the landscape and peoples of these acquisitions'.[7] To see the world thus, as an opposition between 'enterprising' photographers and peoples deemed so passive that they can be 'documented' along with (almost as part of) the landscape, is already to interpret it according to specific historical and cultural assumptions.

Born in Frankfurt in 1845, the son of a customs officer, Lindt arrived in Australia in November 1862, having worked his passage on a Dutch ship. In the same spirit, he took to working his way through the bush, this time by tuning pianos, finally arriving at the town of Grafton, a farming centre on the Clarence River, some 300 miles north of Sydney. The population of Grafton at this time was about two and a half thousand settlers, among them a number of German migrants from the Rhineland and Saxony, who operated vineyards and tobacco plantations. A prominent member of this group was its interpreter, Conrad Wagner, an artist and photographer to whom Lindt became apprenticed for the next five years, and from whom he learnt his photographic skills. In 1867 Lindt visited his parents in Europe, and on 20 September, 1869, following his return to Australia, he took British citizenship. Soon afterwards Wagner retired, and the young Lindt was able to take over the popular business. Early in 1870 he opened a new studio in the town, 'fitted in the best and most complete manner with suitable reception and dressing rooms, and. with the most modern improvements'.[8] Lindt's work included photographing local industry, portraits of houses and their owners, and recording the development of the town. He also took pictures of the Aboriginal people of the area, both in the bush and posed in studio settings. (Examples of these latter photographs were included in the extensive 1988 London Bicentennial exhibition, 'Stories of Australian Art'.[9])

The Australian Aborigines proved a popular subject for photographers, as they had earlier been for painters, but the motives involved and the images produced differed for several reasons. First encounters with the Aborigines had occasioned debate as to whether they were supremely fortunate in their lack of material culture, or hopelessly debased in their lack of any culture at all; European observers tended towards the latter assessment. Few echoed Cook, who wrote in his journal that they were 'happier than we Europeans', for as they were 'wholly unacquainted not only with the superfluous but the necessary Conveniences so much sought after in Europe, they are happy in not knowing the use of them'.[10] Aboriginal people tended to be ignored by settlers when not despised or attacked; paintings included them only as representatives of the lowest stage of human existence. The German anatomist H. Klaatsch, whose belief in evolutionary 'progress' reflected scientific opinion of the day, visited Australia to study Aboriginal origins, and in 1923 pronounced the race to be a 'stationary remnant of primitive humanity'.[11]

Charles Darwin's *The Origin of Species* appeared in 1859, three years before the young Lindt arrived in Australia. The creed of social Darwinism which derived from it strongly reinforced (where it did not directly inspire) the evolutionist tendencies described, and was influential in Australia from about 1870; it dominated cultural attitudes until the 1920s. In land settlement, it fostered 'an ethic of conquest, providing the basic moral justifications for dispossession—those best able to exploit the land, or anything else for that matter, have the best right to it'. In 'high art', it reinforced aesthetic conventions in allotting Aborigines an ever-diminishing role on the Australian scene. The 1880 painting 'Evening Shadows', now in the Art Gallery of South Australia, by the popular artist and photographer H.J. Johnstone, depicted picturesque watery reflections of an Aboriginal encampment, but its subtext was the fading role of the Aboriginal figures. The composition's sunset glow encouraged nostalgic acceptance of the scientifically 'inevitable' through sensitive contemplation of the picturesque. These nineteenth-century landscape images so central to Australian national mythology are usually less explicit than Johnstone's painting, simply omitting the Aborigines altogether. At best the Aboriginal people are depicted as passive spectators of pastoral expansion—the 'opening up' of the land—or as shepherds.[12] In this way the Aborigines were excluded as systematically from the national mythology as they were from the 1901 constitution which proclaimed the seven Australian colonies a nation.[13]

Photography was affected differently from painting by such attitudes, for distinctions were in any case made between what was suitable for depiction in high (graphic) and in low (photographic) art.[14] Aborigines usually qualified for high art only if treated in an ennobling manner, and aesthetic, social and political pressures all discouraged this: to 'record' the predestined fading of an indigenous people before one's own acts of violence and dispossession demands a vision of them as long-suffering, not heroic. Heroism was the prerogative of explorers and settlers. Late nineteenth-century Australian paintings depict Aborigines (if at all) in a generalised manner, encouraging the viewer to extrapolate a moral, rather than be roused by specific wrongs. This was true of many photographs, but photography has several masters, and images of the Aborigines also had the supposedly scientific purpose of accurately recording their likenesses before their extinction. This activity could conveniently overlap with satisfying the demand for views of typical Australian bush life, as increasing urbanisation gave scenes with a pastoral quality (of which Aborigines could be seen as one element) a nostalgic appeal; many of these photographs later circulated widely as postcards.[15] The photographs produced from such mixed motives (scientific, commercial, personal, artistic-nostalgic) constitute a rich and complex body of visual material which has yet to be accorded the scholarly attention necessary for it to be incorporated as cultural heritage. The questions raised are as important as they are diverse, straddling as they often do present academic divisions between history, art history, sociology, anthropology and media studies.

Today Lindt's studio portraits seem more artefacts of camera culture than records of Aboriginal culture.[16] They reveal all too clearly that when we represent others we also, albeit unknowingly, present ourselves; to see a person as a subject for depiction (whether for the purposes of science, art, or entertainment) is to reveal much of one's own intentions. Yet if our perceptions (and so our representations) of others are inevitably self-reflective, most self-perceptions are also to some degree dependent upon the perceptions of others. This process is mutual and largely unconscious in social relationships, except at moments of conflict, but for Australian Aborigines it is fraught because European settlers effected not only widescale destruction of their culture, but also its selective (if random) preservation; fragments selected as interesting are now 'curated' in museums worldwide, while the historical record is short on alternative representations of 'what actually occurred'. Many of these blanks will never be filled; omission was often deliberate, and those who could rectify such omission are long dead.[17] In this situation, no matter how well-intentioned the research, 'the increase of knowledge increases our [white] control. For it is we Europeans who associate antiquity with "a rich cultural heritage" '.[18] In this situation photography offers uniquely valuable images of nineteenth-century Aboriginal and settler culture-contact; Lindt's pictures contribute an important dimension to such a usable past.

Lindt records the New South Wales river town of Grafton in the early 1870s as juxtaposition of frontier harshness and genteel respectability, and his own profession of photographer encompassed a similar range of experience. Photographers at this period needed skill in preparing the chemicals used to coat and fix the glass plates which carried the photographic image; this had to be done on the spot in a portable darkroom (often a small tent). Over and beyond such technical competence, Lindt possessed a sure sense of composition, as well as remarkable entrepreneurial talents. Contemporary accounts suggest that his work was popular with Grafton residents. Towards the end of his stay a local newspaper stressed that he had 'ever made it his study to raise the standard of photography, and thereby create a taste for artistic productions', an aim in which the writer felt he had been 'signally successful'. The article noted that 'few houses in the district' did not contain 'some of his gems', a reminder that photographs had long been important domestic icons.[19] If Grafton's residents in the 1870s valued Lindt's 'artistic' depiction of their surroundings, those selfsame photographs today constitute the best visual evidence we have of the town's appearance at that time.

In about 1872, some thirty prints of Lindt's work at Grafton were gathered together as *Clarence River Views*. This album is invaluable in that it is the choice of the photographer himself, rather than that of a subsequent editor.[20] It is also a reminder of the extent to which, throughout his career in Australia, Lindt's role was to represent others. At Grafton he was a recent immigrant, photographing a relatively small community in which he worked for 13 years. In Melbourne after 1876 he was again a newcomer, this time establishing a reputation with the wealthy and fashionable (partly that of the foreigner, it seems) which he later exploited in running his select guest house 'The Hermitage' at Healesville, in the wooded hills on the northern outskirts of Melbourne. In 1885 he visited New Guinea, an area which then had strong German colonial links, in the role (at his own shrewd suggestion) of Official Photographer to the British expedition of annexation led by Sir Peter Scratchley, the first British Special Commissioner.[21]

For the modern viewer, the sense of 'otherness' in Lindt's photographs derives partly from their formal quality. The lengthy exposures necessary, the prevailing social and aesthetic conventions, and Lindt's tendency to compose in a painterly manner gave them a highly posed look. At the theoretical level his writings show his awareness of the role that the camera could—and should—play in recording as accurately as possible the events of contemporary history.[22] In 'View just above Lawrence' Lindt's camera records the winding Clarence river, but focuses on the reassuring evidence of settlement. This ranges from the ring-barked forest in the background through rough sheds and a bark hut to the gabled homestead in the foreground, on whose verandah an elegant couple stand. Mere 'information' perhaps, but it is indeed an artist-photographer who selects a high viewpoint (so high that its location is a puzzle) which places these details in a long perspective linked by the river's curve. The picture invites admiration for the carefully-contrived and maintained limits of material civilisation amid a vast and indifferent landscape; its Australian painterly equivalents are the early nineteenth-century topographical paintings of Joseph Lycett and John Eyre. A recent 'study in spatial history' offers a stimulating reading of similar photographs of settlement, and argues that, like imperial history's invention of the heroic pioneer, such pictures have been 'treated as if the settler took them, as if he made the picturesque, and not vice versa'. A true history of photography, 'would have to do primarily, not with the visible content, but with the invisible point of view, the "here" on which "there" was dialectically predicated'.[23] That such differences of literal and social position operated even within Lindt's professional round at Grafton is suggested by his photograph 'English Church and Parsonage, Glenn Innes' (*illus. 8*) the sturdy wooden bridge and stone church buildings reflect the confidence communicated by the self-possessed and proprietorial gentlemen in the foreground; manual workers (perhaps resting as much as posing) are suitably distanced on the far side of the bridge.[24]

Lindt's Aboriginal studies in *Clarence River Views* are of special interest. The *Sydney Morning Herald* commented in 1874 that there was 'no settled portion of our colony' which offered 'a better field for the study of original bush life' than that of the northern rivers: 'the blacks preserve their customs and traditions, adhering more closely to true aboriginal life than tribes in the other districts of New South Wales'. The paper complimented Lindt on 'the artistic use' made of what it termed 'the rugged subjects he has had at his disposal'. His photographs were praised as 'faithful likenesses and fine examples of Aboriginal bush life in Australia', and one market envisaged by Lindt for his album is indicated by the correspondent's remark that as 'a souvenir from Australia to friends in Europe' it would 'be acceptable to many'.[25]

For an overseas market all the images in Lindt's album—indeed, all images of Australia—would be 'other', and by that token exotic: Lindt sent a copy of to the London *Illustrated News*, no doubt hoping it would be reviewed, and engravings of it printed, but he was to be disappointed. In 1875 he issued a second album, *Aboriginal Natives of the Clarence*

River District, NSW, entirely devoted to Aboriginal portraits (*illus. 9 and 10*). This collection contains studio portraits characterised by an artificiality (studied pose, painted backdrop, token artefacts) which jars both against what we consider a more appropriate style for such subjects, and against what we now take to be the proper role of photography (as opposed to painting). Almost every word here needs quotation marks ('artificiality', 'natural', 'appropriate', 'proper') for each begs important questions. Like other media, photography imposes its own set of cultural grids through which it records, and we perceive, its 'subject': there is no unmediated access to reality. It is to these perceptual questions, as they affect the production and interpretation of Lindt's photographs, that I now turn.

Photography plays a key role in selling yesteryear's face to today's consumer markets, and has even been accused of not so much recording as inventing the past. Such questions affect especially the interest in 'old photographs of vanished peoples and crowded, dusty cases of 'primitive-artefacts with faded labels'; today such discussion is as likely to be found in a stylish article on *objets trouvés* and interior decor as in discussion of photographic or museum theory.[26] Photographs taken in the past (and especially 'old photographs of vanished peoples') seem to carry that peculiarly photographic guarantee of authenticity, an assurance that this really was how things were on the day when these long-dead individuals posed before the lens. Such trust finds classic expression in the passport photograph, by which we 'prove' our identity to anonymous officials. It is inconceivable that anyone (government agent or simple citizen alike) would now trust a painted portrait of the passport bearer, no matter how faithful the likeness. Passport photographs are often misleading (or outdated), but trust of the medium outweighs any shortcomings of a particular image.[27]

Lindt's Grafton photographs of Aborigines are problematical because they exemplify conventions at variance not only with those now employed, but also within themselves. The group photographs of Aborigines taken in the bush are, of course, posed by the photographer, but the poses largely accord with photographic conventions familiar to us (not least from our own snapshots) and so do not obtrude. A commentator observed in 1874 that they 'represent very faithfully aboriginals, male and female, of all ages, as the traveller finds them in the wilds, and *not as if just prepared for portraiture*'. Quite apart from the implied contrast with painting, it is possible that this comment also made reference to Lindt's studio photographs of Aboriginals (to appear in the 1875 album) in which the subjects are very much 'prepared for portraiture'. The phrase quoted is taken from a promotional pamphlet of approving critical comments assembled by Lindt himself in Melbourne during the late 1880s; possibly by then he sought to distance his early work from subsequent (and cruder) studio portraits of Aboriginal people by other photographers.[28]

Lindt's studio portraits are today both valuable and problematic, their seeming mismarriage of 'content' and 'style' provoking a wider consideration of the problems of representing others. A contemporary example illustrates what is at issue here. In 1988 a British television documentary used several of Lindt's Aboriginal studio portraits from the 1875 Grafton album in precisely the way that their highly conventional nature might be thought to render impossible; namely, as illustrations of the condition to which Aboriginal people were reduced by the time the photographs were taken in the late nineteenth century. This emphasis was surprising since the programme (by the Australian reporter John Pilger) was specifically concerned with the impact of white settlement on Australia's Aboriginal people; Lindt's images are invaluable photographic *examples* of that impact, not raw 'evidence'.[29] They illustrate process, not product.

A comparable example of graphic images being read according to inappropriate conventions is discussed in a recent study of eighteenth-century neo-classical culture in New South Wales, where early topographical paintings usually seen as charming but incompetent attempts at accurate depiction are reassessed as precise and complex studies in 'the picturesque and the cult of associationism'. This fresh evaluation suggests that 'the justification for these liberties with nature was the high value placed upon "mood", "character", "harmony" and "expression" in the interpretation of landscape'. Lindt, in his comments on his 1885 New Guinea photographs (and specifically on the role of photography in exploration), was emphatic that 'artistic photography' was 'the legitimate and proper means' for showing what 'foreign lands and their inhabitants look like', rather than 'drawings, either partly or purely imaginary'.[30] This could stand as a defence of the photographic, as against the graphic, image but for the term 'artistic', for Lindt an assertion of photography's status vis-a-vis painting. A further complication is that while we might agree that photography, no less than painting, demands special—if different—skills, Lindt's studio portraits of Aborigines employ painterly conventions of posing, and include painted backgrounds. Their 'artistic' qualities now seem as 'unphotographic' as they are 'unrealistic' (for us the two terms are often synonymous). Yet to dismiss Lindt's studio photographs as little more than inaccurate representations of Aboriginal culture is as unhelpful as accepting them as evidence of Aboriginal living conditions in the 1870s.

A working theoretical approach to such photographs is needed, and Nicholas Peterson has posited three ideological contexts—romanticism, realism and the documentary; these are not mutually exclusive in principle, and are rarely so in practice. The dominant mode, romanticism, reflects 'the belief that the camera reveals the world of essences which connects it with the world of art'. This approach links the romantic mode with 'a belief in idealism and a redemptive ideology'. The realistic mode expresses 'the popular view that photographs capture the world as it is'. Photography, on this analysis, 'is assumed not to transform the objects it records but merely present them to our scrutiny'. The third context, that of the documentary, reflects 'the belief that photographs can have a practical effect on everyday life', and depends heavily on 'captions or accompanying prose that attempt to firm up the political and moral associations of the image'; this emphasis on complementary information makes it clear that photographs cannot serve as uncontaminated evidence.[31]

Lindt's studio portraits of Aborigines would fall within Peterson's romantic framework, resolving as they do 'contradictory feelings towards other cultures by transforming them into aesthetic phenomena and in so doing decontextualising and distancing them'. Some such codification of the aestheticising and distancing conventions in these photographs (those elements we find most 'dated') is essential for us to accept the images as a cultural and historical resource; without it they will be neglected, if for no better reason than embarrassment. Indeed, it has been suggested that 'the "nearness" of the photograph to reality', and ways in which 'both photography and the western appropriation of tribal man brought distant things close', created the need in the late nineteenth century for 'framing' conventions to accommodate otherwise intolerable juxtapositions.[32] In his studio portraits Lindt uses devices (studio setting, painted backdrop and 'typical' accoutrements) which invite attention to generalities of Aboriginal life beyond the image, rather than to specific details of a particular print. As with the example of earlier topographical paintings, such devices can be seen as indicators of the appropriate response required of the viewer; in both cases, it would seem, our erroneous assumption tends to be that realism is necessarily the convention within which the image operates. The tendency to make this assumption is specially strong with photography.

If Lindt's portraits might be classified in Peterson's taxonomy as romantic, our own preferred mode of depiction for native peoples is assuredly 'realistic', that is, characterised by 'a sense of solemnity' and willing belief in 'full disclosure of the subject's nature'. In this convention the posing accordingly 'underlines the empiricist ideology with its emphasis on concreteness—all is exposed to be seen—and immersion in the present social reality'. Any embarrassment at our own consumption of other cultures and peoples (whether by imperialism, capitalism or tourism) is accordingly—and ironically—assuaged by 'concerned' photographs or films. These media encourage the illusion of direct ('un-mediated') contact with the people depicted at the same time as they declare their 'objectivity', and unsentimental detachment, in representing them as other. In practice, many photographs of Aborigines (and of other 'primitive' peoples) convey the impression that they 'have surrendered to the camera and been subjugated by it'.[33] Patronising (if well meaning) concern is easily evoked where conventional coding reinforces the 'information' of the image; so, television reports of (yet another . . .) drought in Africa, presented by a duly concerned 'newscaster' and depicting the passive forms of starving 'natives' may simply reinforce our sense of distance—geographical and moral—from such events. Not least because we will be duly 'returned' to the studio (as if we had ever left the comfort of our home).

Another illuminating context for Lindt's Aboriginal portraits is provided by several similar studies by him of typical bush types, including the prospector, the shearer and the swagman. Though these photographs may have been taken at Grafton it is significant that Lindt also used them in albums issued in the late 1870s or early 1880s, when he operated from a city-centre studio in Melbourne. The phenomenal expansion of urban Melbourne in the latter half of the nineteenth century provided both a motive and a market for idealized images of rural life, and Lindt rarely missed an opportunity.[34] Such photographs parallel favourite subjects of the Heidelberg painters at the same period, depicting as they do that outback and pioneering activity which (according to the nascent white settler mythology) was characteristic of Australian national life. As with the Aboriginal portraits, the painted backdrop is of mountain scenery, and again great attention is paid to the inclusion of appropriate gear: pick, shovel and panning dish for the digger; bedroll—or 'matilda'—and billycan for the swaggie, who is supposedly 'caught' while on the move, whereas the shearer and digger face the camera directly. An 1876 review referred to these studies usefully as 'pictures of character . . . in what the artist terms the "genre" style'. The Melbourne *Argus* found the groups 'most artistically arranged, representing scenes of camp life, sheep-shearing, hunting, &c' and could

Johannes Lindt

not speak too highly of 'the execution of these photographs'. A note in the 1883 Melbourne Exhibition programme also refers to Lindt's 'genre work', and gives a detailed description of one example:

> The picture represents a bush traveller . . . weary after his day's toil, camped at the road-side enjoying his pannikin of tea; his swag and digger's tools are lying down near to him, and, as evening seems about to close, he has evidently made up his mind to camp for the night.[35]

The ease with which the writer constructs a narrative for the picture suggests one function of such images, notwithstanding what we see as their decidedly static quality. Each carefully-located detail offered opportunities for the viewer to become involved with the scene and 'character' depicted, each item and incident forming part of a well-known and accepted repertoire, upon which individual imagination could play.

In Australian nineteenth-century paintings, according to Maynard, Aborigines 'are normally represented . . . by portrait heads' rather than by scenes in which they are 'engaged in social or practical activities such as hunting or fishing'. While 'photographers and illustrators often represent Aboriginal ceremonies', painters 'virtually ignore them'.[36] If this is so, Lindt's studio portraits, applying as they do the same pictorial conventions to both settler and Aboriginal subjects, offer a rare opportunity to compare images of Australian life usually segregated as severely in art as in experience. Moreover, in one instance Lindt has provided rich grounds for analysis by thriftily framing a portrait of a digger on a mount which carries the printed series title 'Australian Aboriginals'. The word 'Aboriginals' has been neatly deleted, and in some cases 'Scenery' written in, but both terms remain visible as bizarrely 'alternative' captions for an heroic figure of white mythology (*illus. 11*). Yet while Aboriginal portraits were accommodated (repressively) under just such photographic series titles as 'Characteristic Australian Scenery', Lindt's white frontier characters resist depiction as 'Australian Aboriginals'. This double-titled image poignantly expresses the irreconcilable conflict of perceptions underlying the apparent genre similarity of these photographs. The very concept of 'genre' forms part of the dominant perceptual code, which requires deletion of 'Aboriginals' in the photograph illustrated—not because it might offend Aboriginal sensibilities, but because it definitely subverts white Australian codes of representation.

By the 1880s Lindt's reputation in the best Melbourne circles was

95

well established, and his work at Grafton and Melbourne prior to 1885 would ensure him a place in the history of Australian photography, but his most outstanding pictures were still to come. They were the results of his 1885 trip to New Guinea with Sir Peter Scratchley's expedition of annexation: *Picturesque New Guinea*, published in London in 1887, its text superbly illustrated with fifty Autotype photographic prints of the new colony's life and scenery (*illus. 12*). In the Preface to this book Lindt argued that science should adopt 'photographic methods for making its graphic records', and specifically criticised many book illustrations (including those in some scientific texts) for being 'a vehicle of personal expression', rather than a matter of fact. In the opening chapter, he wrote: 'It seemed to me that a goal I had long been striving to reach was now in sight, and that I was fortunate enough . . . to be the humble means of communicating truthful information to others'. At the same time, he complained in the Preface that 'when perusing the accounts of exploring expeditions' he had 'always noticed with a pang of disappointment' that however carefully the staff was chosen, 'it was, as a rule, considered sufficient to supply one of the members with a mahogany camera, lens, and chemicals to make pictures'.[37]

Lindt envisaged his own role in New Guinea very differently. He saw his photographs in *Picturesque New Guinea* as both factual records and 'artistic'; in similar vein, the Melbourne *Argus* wrote that many of its 'accurate representations' were 'beautiful as pictures, *irrespective of their unavoidable fidelity* as transcripts of natural objects'. In Sydney the book's 'picturesque scenes' were acclaimed as 'selected with a fine sense of the artistic too rarely exhibited by those who make the camera a medium for the reproduction of landscape'. Interest in a neighbouring 'exotic' land and its inhabitants was one factor in the book's appeal. It was described as 'a photo-panorama of that strange place' because of its informative and immediate style: 'Mr Lindt . . . has seen the strange people and strange places with the eye of an artist, and, by the aid of his camera, has seized them. His book shows us New Guinea as it is'. This stress upon the viewer being able to see a 'strange place' in photographs which present it 'as it is' indicates what, on our earlier classification, would be a realistic interpretation of Lindt's pictures (that is, according to Peterson, photography assumed 'not to transform the objects it records but merely present them to our view'). Reference to the way Lindt has 'seized' the places and people of New Guinea, on the other hand, accords with the view that the photographic medium facilitates a detachment from its subject more violent than 'artistic': to 'shoot' people is one way of avoiding more demanding relationships.

Lindt's role as Official Photographer to an expedition of imperial annexation offers the perfect context for such an interpretation, although it seems that the phrase quoted sought to stress the *immediacy* of the pictures. The same commentator concludes with a documentary emphasis upon the value of Lindt's New Guinea pictures ('the belief', in Peterson's words, 'that photographs can have a practical effect on everyday life') and suggests that such 'a vast amount of [visual] information' should be available 'on the table of every student, and in the catalogue of every Mechanics' Institute in Australia'.[38]

In December 1888 the *Scotsman* reviewed *Picturesque New Guinea*, and from its distant perspective agreed that 'the art of photography' had never been applied 'on so liberal a scale, or with such brilliant results' to the illustration of travel as in this book. It felt that Lindt's photographs, with their blend of 'artistic beauty and fidelity as transcripts from nature', did not 'merely illustrate New Guinea' but suggested 'a new and more excellent way of "bringing home" tropical and other scenery'. In placing the phrase 'bringing home' in inverted commas the reviewer may have sought to suggest its double meaning: not only is New Guinea made more real, but is also brought home (albeit in photographic form) to a base both metropolitan and imperial. For the modern reader comparison with a photographic safari is inevitable, and by no means irrelevant. Subjugation by the advanced technology of the camera is but one aspect of imperial expansion, and the pleasurable 'possession' and contemplation of distant and exotic countries in photographic form both reflects and reaffirms an imperial world view.[39]

Such 'bringing home' of photographic (among other) trophies to the family drawing room was an important cultural aspect of empire, in which literature also played a role. In its comments on Lindt's book the *Sydney Morning Herald* stressed the ability of photography to 'divest New Guinea of that atmosphere of dim mystery that appeals to the imagination like one of Rider Haggard's powerful stories'. The photographer, it claimed, 'lifts the curtain of illusive uncertainty like a veil', and when we look at his pictures 'there is nothing left to the imagination any more'. Such enthusiasm mingles a thrill at previously hidden secrets with stress upon the privileged nature of the photograph in a way which perhaps reaffirms, rather than corrects, Haggard's interest in the revelation of 'dim mystery'.[40] One Melbourne journal felt that the reader of Lindt's book was carried 'from village to village', so that New Guinea was 'no longer a dark and mysterious island' but (at least as regards 'the British portion of it') 'a familiar and desirable country'. These carefully balanced terms ('dark'/'familiar', 'island'/'country') reflect the perception of another culture as Other, and the patronising tone informs the praise of Lindt's photographs for the way in which they 'familiarise us with the Papuans and their interesting country', even making it possible for us 'to read their thoughts and trace their characters in the expressions of their faces'. One review applauded the 'tact and fore-thought' evidenced in Lindt's book, noting that the forethought included the realisation that there were excellent commercial prospects for such a handsome volume on this unknown land.[41]

Much of the excitement over Lindt's book derived from the technical quality of its photographic reproductions which, said one reviewer, left 'an impression on the reader's mind of actual contact with the subjects'. The impact such images had is suggested by a comparison with another publication that year which (apparently without permission) used Lindt's photographs as the basis for engraved illustrations; *Pioneering in New Guinea* by the Reverend James Chalmers. The photograph chosen by Lindt as the frontispiece for his own book was 'Motu Water Carrier, Port Moresby' (*illus. 13*), a picture which shrewdly combined ethnographical interest with picturesque landscape scenery (and, no doubt, a certain exotic/erotic thrill). These interrelated appeals of the image inform the Melbourne *Chronicle*'s enthusiasm for 'the lithe figure of the girl full of ease . . . standing out with great force from the background of palm trees and undulating country'. The engraving reproduced in Chalmers' book, by comparison, lacks all sense of setting: hard outlines emphasise the lack of perspective, and the wooden figure floats against a seemingly flat backdrop.[42]

The difference between the two images is not limited to one of definition. If Lindt's assertion of the need for the photographic depiction of native lands required proof, comparison of his woman's delicately-shadowed face with the harshly-lit and Europeanised features of the engraving would suffice. Such a tendency is further revealed in another Chalmers engraving derived from a Lindt photograph, 'Native Teachers' (*illus. 14*). The original captures the strange formality of the scene, its figures posed against the flag of a supposedly benevolent imperialism; in the engraving the faces of the native teachers are again Europeanised, and the 'strangeness' of the background detail is lost. Chalmers' depiction of education and Empire appropriates the very landscape and its people in a European mode of vision. Despite its formal conventions, Lindt's picture still allows a reading which illuminates the process of cultural, as well as political, annexation; the engraving is as didactic as its subject matter.

The importance of Lindt's New Guinea photographs has not yet been recognised. Striking though they are as early Australian images of this 'primitive' land, it is his studio 'photographs of character' that have proved more amenable to the Australian legend, and which have been most reproduced, together with his (now nostalgic) views of Victorian Melbourne.[43] Properly understood, Lindt's unique achievement in *Picturesque New Guinea* forms part not only of the history of empire but also of that photographic record in which a nation may confront with fresh awareness aspects of its past. In this sense his photographs record not a chance venture by an enterprising German-born migrant into an exotic land somewhere to the north of Australia, but an early example of Australia's involvement (first as a group of British colonies, later as a powerful tutelary power) with what is increasingly recognised as her own 'near north' rather than (Britain's) 'Far East'. Australia's role in Pacific history since 1885—and especially since the Second World War—has only enhanced the historical importance of Lindt's New Guinea photographs, and their potential to inform readings of Australian art. If they continue to be seen as irrelevant, or at best marginal, to Australia's national mythology, that mythology itself will be accordingly impoverished.

NOTES

1. Richard White, *Inventing Australia: Images and Identity 1968–1980* (Sydney, 1981), p.ix.
2. This is a principle of general importance insufficiently recognised in academic life. For another rewarding examination of the issue in an Australian context see John Docker's *In A Critical Condition* (Ringwood, Victoria, 1984); the final chapter is a wonderfully entertaining (and sobering) account of the personal cost of differing theoretical structures. For broader studies, see Terry Eagleton, *Literary Theory, An Introduction* (Oxford, 1983), especially Chapter 1, and Edward W. Said *The World, The Text, and the Critic* (1983; London, 1984).
3. For useful discussion on Australian art in these terms see, for example: Bernard Smith *The Death of the Artist as Hero: Essays in History and Culture* (Melbourne, 1988); Graeme Turner, *National Fictions: Literature, Film and the Construction of Australian Narrative* (Sydney, 1986); John Fiske, Bob Hodge, Graeme Turner, *Myths of Oz: Reading Australian Popular Culture* (Sydney, 1987); Ian Burn, Nigel Lendon, Charles Merewether, Ann Stephen, *The Necessity of Australian Art: An Essay about Interpretation* (Sydney, 1988).
4. For film, see Turner, *National Fictions*. The best historical account of Australian photography is the catalogue produced by Gael Newton for the

1988 Australian Bicentennial exhibition at the Australian National Gallery, Canberra, *Shades of Light: Photography and Australia 1839–1988* (Sydney, 1988).

5. The most recent study of Lindt is Shar Jones's *J.W. Lindt Master Photographer* (Melbourne, 1985). While providing useful fresh information on Lindt's life and work, this study does nothing to further assessment of Lindt's photographs in the context of the Australian visual arts. More useful discussions are: Helen Topliss, *The Artists' Camps: Plein Air Painting in Melbourne 1885-1898* (Melbourne, 1984); Leigh Astbury, *City Bushmen: The Heidelberg School and Rural Mythology* (Melbourne, 1985); and (on painting only) Tim Bonyhady, *Images in Opposition: Australian Landscape Painting 1801-1890* (Melbourne, 1985).

6. For invaluable material on visual depictions of the Australian Aborigines (in painting and in photography) see Ian and Tamsin Donaldson (eds.), *Seeing the First Australians* (Sydney, 1985).

7. Peter Lyon, 'The role of the photographer' in *Commonwealth in Focus: 130 Years of Photographic History*, (1982), p.9.

8. Information on Lindt from Jones, *J.W. Lindt*; quotation from the *Clarence and Richmond Examiner*, 25 January 1870, quoted in Jones, p.3.

9. See Jonathan Watkins, *Stories of Australian Art* (London, 1988).

10. The best introduction to this issue remains Bernard Smith, *European Vision and the South Pacific* (1960); second revised edition (New Haven and London, 1985). For Cook, see Glyndwr Williams, 'Reactions on Cook's Voyage', in Donaldson, *Seeing the First Australians*, pp.35-50.

11. See Henry Reynolds, 'Breaking the Great Australian Silence: Aborigines in Australian Historiography 1955-1983', in Peter Quartermaine, ed., *Diversity Itself: Essays in Australian Arts and Culture* (Exeter, 1986), pp.39-50. Klaatsch quoted in D.J. Mulvaney, 'The Darwinian Perspective', in Donaldson, *Seeing the First Australians*, pp.68-75. Reference on p.69.

12. Bernard Smith, *The Spectre of Truganini*, 1980 Boyer Lectures (Sydney, n.d. 1980), p.15. See Bonyhady, *Images in Opposition*, especially Chapter 3, pp.40-59.

13. See J. Reynolds, *The Other Side of the Frontier* (Ringwood, Victoria, 1982), and White, *Inventing Australia*, Chapter 7, pp.110-24.

14. See Astbury, *City Bushmen*; interestingly, Bonyhady's ('art') book, *Images in Opposition*, makes no mention of photography, though, as Astbury shows, it was photographs which disseminated the dominant images of the period.

15. See Margaret Maynard, 'Projections of Melancholy', and Nicolas Peterson, 'The Popular Image', in Donaldson, *Seeing the First Australians*, pp.92-109 and pp.164-80 respectively.

16. In *J.W. Lindt* Jones reproduces (p.8) a revealing photograph of Lindt's studio in Hawthorn, Melbourne, complete with framed prints of his New Guinea photographs amid the potted plants, bearskins, stuffed birds and damasks. Typically, she offers no analysis whatsoever of this image.

17. See Ian and Tamsin Donaldson, 'First Sight', in their *Seeing the First*

Australians, pp.15-20. For a personal (white) account of imaginative response to this gap in history, see Judith Wright *A Cry For the Dead* (Melbourne, 1981).

18. Paul Carter, *The Road to Botany Bay* (London, 1987), p.xviii.
19. *Grafton and Clarence River Examiner*, 2 September 1876, quoted in Lindt, *A Few Results of Modern Photography* (Melbourne, 1886), p.16.
20. The only copy of this album—which was overlooked by Jones—is held in the Pictorial Reading Room at the National Library, Canberra.
21. See Jack Cato, *The Story of the Camera in Australia*, (Melbourne, 1955), and Jones, *J.W. Lindt*.
22. See Lindt's Preface to *Picturesque New Guinea, accompanied with fifty full-page Autotype illustrations from negatives of Portraits from life and groups and landscapes from nature by J.W. Lindt FRGS* (London: Longmans, 1887).
23. Paul Carter, *The Road to Botany Bay*, p.246.
24. Sometimes his picturesque arrangement of a view can strike a discordant note, as in *Australian Meat Company's Works*, where a foreground figure (however useful for scale), evokes pastoral conventions quite at odds with what is, despite the rural setting, a photograph of industrial plant.
25. *Sydney Morning Herald*, 24 November 1874, quoted in Lindt, *Results*, p.14.
26. Susan Sontag, *On Photography* (1977; Harmondsworth, 1979), p.67; see Jill Lloyd, 'Old Photographs, Vanished Peoples and Stolen Potatoes', *Art Monthly* (London, 1985), pp.13-6; for a rich and entertaining introduction to uses of the past, see David Lowenthal, *The Past is a Foreign Country* (Cambridge, 1985).
27. See Roland Barthes, *Camera Lucida: Reflections on Photography*, translated by Richard Howard (1980; London, 1984); and Paul Fussell, *Abroad: British Literary Traveling Between the Wars* (New York, 1980).
28. Lindt, *Results*, p.7, my emphasis.
29. 'Secrets', Part Two of *The Last Dream*, screened on ITV on January 19, 1988.
30. Robert Dixon, *The Course of Empire: Neo-Classical Culture in New South Wales 1788-1860* (Melbourne, 1986), pp.47-8. Lindt, Preface to *Picturesque New Guinea*, pp.vii-viii.
31. Peterson, 'The Popular Image', pp.165-6.
32. Peterson, 'The Popular Image', p.165. See Lloyd, 'Old Photographs'.
33. Peterson, 'The Popular Image', p.174.
34. Jones, *J.W. Lindt*, pp.6-7. Examples are reproduced here and in Cato. See also Graeme Davidson, *The Rise and Fall of Marvellous Melbourne* (Melbourne, 1978), especially Chapter 10, pp.229-57.
35. *Brisbane Courier*, September, 1876; Melbourne *Argus*, 11 May 1877; and the catalogue for the 1883 Melbourne Exhibition; all quoted in *Results*, pp.16-9.
36. See Maynard, 'Projections of Melancholy', p.94
37. *Picturesque New Guinea*, ps.vii, viii, 13, and vii.
38. Melbourne *Argus*, December 1885; Sydney *Bulletin*, 14 April 1888; *Weekly*

Times; all quoted in Lindt, *Notes*, ps.16 (my emphasis), 32 and 29 respectively.

39. *The Scotsman*, 20 December 1888, quoted Lindt, *Notes*, p.36. See, for example, the essays in John MacKenzie (ed.), *Imperialism and Popular Culture* (Manchester, 1986) and the provocative documentary film directed by Dennis O'Rourke, *Cannibal Tours*(1987).

40. *Sydney Morning Herald*, quoted Lindt, *Notes*, p.30. For an imaginative exploration of literature in this vein, see Martin Green, *Dreams of Adventure, Deeds of Empire* (London, 1980).

41. Melbourne *Daily Telegraph*; and Melbourne *Age*, 7 January 1888; quoted in Lindt, *Notes*, ps.28 and 29.

42. *Sydney Morning Herald*, quoted in Lindt, *Notes*, p.30; The Rev. James Chalmers, *Pioneering in New Guinea* (London, 1887). *Chronicle*, quoted Lindt, *Notes*, p.23.

43. Examples are printed in Cato, *The Story of the Camera in Australia*. Almost every photographic picture book since 1900 has used material by Lindt.

MICK GIDLEY

Edward S. Curtis' Indian Photographs:
A National Enterprise

Edward S. Curtis' *The North American Indian* (1907–1930) is a justi-
fiably famous set of 20 volumes of illustrated text and 20 portfolios
of large-size photogravures devoted to over eighty different Native
American peoples living west of the Mississippi and Missouri rivers
who, in Curtis' prefatory words, 'still retained to a considerable degree
their primitive customs and traditions'. On July 27, 1924, when fourteen
of the volumes had been published, Curtis delivered a lecture in Santa
Fé, New Mexico, in which, before going on to other matters, he gave
an accurate summary of the coverage and concerns of *The North
American Indian*: 'the old time Indian, his dress, his ceremonies, his life
and manners'. To head off the pictorial aspect of the project Curtis chose
his 1904 image, 'The Vanishing Race'. According to its caption, 'the
thought which this picture is meant to convey is that the Indians as a
race, already shorn of their . . . strength and stripped of their primitive
dress, are passing into the darkness of an unknown future'.[1] The image
depicts a line of mounted Navajos riding away from the camera—
receding in perspective—to be swallowed in the deep shadows of cañon
walls. One figure turns in the saddle to look back, as if in regret.
     In Curtis' images Indians would often perform the graphic equivalent
of riding into the darkness of an unknown future. In 'Homeward' (1898),
for instance, taken on Puget Sound, the region in which Curtis had come
of age, some local Indians, their precise physical features lost in shadow,
presumably at the end of a fishing trip, paddle their canoe in the evening
dusk under a slightly threatening sky. In one of his archetypal Plains
photographs—which I would contend have been replicated in countless
westerns—a mounted figure in a glorious feathered headdress has reined
his white horse before a slightly reflecting pool—an 'Oasis in the
Badlands' (1904)—as the twilight comes on (*illus. 15*). Curtis concentrated on representing 'traditional' ways, even to the extent of issuing

wigs to cover shorn hair, providing costumes, and removing signs of the mechanistic twentieth century.

The project was indeed primarily an enterprise of salvage ethnology, concerned to record traditional mores before—as it was assumed they would—they passed away. The collection of ethnological data—including movie footage, thousands of sound recordings and, of course, the photographs—was achieved by a (changing) team of ethnologists, Indian assistants and informants, photographic technicians and others. The production and distribution of the text, which became the responsibility of a specially created business company, The North American Indian Inc., with its head office on Fifth Avenue in New York, involved prodigious organisation, massive funding from the financier J. Pierpont Morgan, and considerable attention to publicity. *The North American Indian*, which included over two thousand photogravures and millions of words, was sold on a subscription basis—mostly to extremely wealthy individuals, but also to major libraries—in a severely limited edition of luxuriously beautiful, leather-bound books. The project, which also led to the production of the very first feature-length narrative documentary film, gave rise to attendant photographic exhibitions, popular magazine articles, lectures, and, as I noted in the Introduction to this book, even a spectacular 'picture opera'. It almost certainly constitutes the largest anthropological enterprise ever undertaken.[2]

And the emphasis we have discerned in 'The Vanishing Race' held true for all of the media to which Curtis contributed, including his popular book titled, tellingly, *Indian Days of the Long Ago* (1914). 'In other words', Curtis continued his 1924 lecture, 'in that work I suppose I am to be classed along with that group . . . occasionally referred to as "long-hairs", those who are interested only in the old Indian, [with] no interest whatsoever in the economic welfare of the Indian now, his education and future'. This was a position Curtis was generally keen to deny, and on this occasion he went on to outline in particular some of the activities of the Indian Welfare League, of which he held the Chair. In fact, for the project such a sharp distinction between 'the old Indian' and the present was, of course, never tenable. Almost all the fieldwork was conducted, with official permission, on reservation lands controlled by the policies of the government of the United States—or, in certain instances, of Canada. An extensive network of contacts at every echelon, from Secretaries of the Interior—even Presidents—down through Commissioners of Indian Affairs to agents on individual reservations was established. At the most humdrum level, the project was frequently in touch with the Bureau of Indian Affairs—for letters of introduction to agents, for copies of Annual Reports, and the like—and the nature of the patronage under which the publication was produced frequently led its principal organiser to flatter figures in positions of power.

The dominant assumption of the Bureau of Indian Affairs in the last decades of the nineteenth century and the first decades of the twentieth century was that Indians should be assimilated into mainstream (that is, white) society as rapidly as possible. It was recognised that different tribes and individuals would proceed towards this goal at varying paces, and that some, because of material circumstances, historical inheritance, or whatever, would have great difficulty adjusting to the new order. Assimilation meant necessarily that Indians should be de-tribalised, encouraged to see themselves not as members of a pre-existing group with traditional practices but as participants in a larger society governed by American laws. The principal instrument intended to achieve this result was the General Allotment or Dawes Act of 1887, which provided for the gradual elimination of collective ownership of reservation lands and the establishment of holdings by individual allotees. These individual property holders, if they so wished, could even sell the land allotted to them—and, in any case, the 'surplus' reservation land was thrown open for white settlement. Indian owners of individual allotments were encouraged to take up United States citizenship—though this did not usually mean they were granted a vote, in that as citizens they were subject to the franchise laws of the particular state in which they resided, most of which discriminated against Indians in this as in other civil rights.

However wrongheaded this set of objectives may now seem, and though it was definitely advocated by some interests as a cynical means of acquiring Indian lands, it was broadly supported by so-called 'Friends of the Indian', such as the Indian Rights Association, with reforming zeal. It held hegemonic status until the twenties—until, in fact, just about that moment when, as Curtis put it in his 1924 lecture, there seemed to be 'an unusual, or abnormal interest in the Indian subject'.[3] In line with these assumptions, the Bureau was dedicated to (i) basic guardianship of those Indians deemed to need health care, provision of rations under treaty obligations, Bureau policing, etc; (ii) allotment of reservation lands, a lengthy legal process involving surveying and conveyancing of millions of acres; and (iii) the progressive acquisition by Indians of US citizenship.

While Curtis' interests in 'the old time' and 'the future' were definitely not divided 'fifty-fifty', as he claimed they were in 1924, from just after he began to photograph Indians his work led him almost inexorably to represent them politically—and/or what he saw as their interests—and thus to intersect with the Indian Bureau in each of the areas sketched above. The project's visual and other representations of Indians can only be adequately understood within the context of official attitudes and policies. Curtis himself, in the 1924 speech, asserted that he was 'strengthened' in his 'welfare work' for present day Indians by his 'ethnological knowledge', and this may well have been the case; what I hope to show here is that the project's ethnological activities were certainly informed by Indian Office beliefs and practices which, in turn, were consistent with the cultural assumptions of the dominant forces in American society. All told, there was a much closer correspondence between such assumptions and the North American Indian project than might at first be apparent.

Let us look at a sample of encounters as displayed in just five incidents. In the first, in 1905, even before the project as such got under way the following year, on returning from a trip to the Southwest, Curtis told Commissioner Francis E. Leupp of conditions among the Havasupai:

> While in the Grand Cañon country I heard considerable of the destitute condition of the Hava supai, owing to the washouts in Cataract Cañon. I gave a little time to learning what I could of their condition, and I am convinced that it is one of these rare cases where help from some source is absolutely necessary. Whether it is possible for the Department to help, is something of which I have no knowledge, but I thought in the interest of humanity, I would send word to let you know how it looked to me.

Curtis had visited the Havasupai in 1903 in what the second volume of *The North American Indian*, published in 1908, rightly described as 'the strangest dwelling place of any tribe in America': the floor of the chasm of the Grand Cañon. There, three thousand feet below the surface of the Cañon, the 'Blue Water People' subsisted on the produce of carefully tended fruit trees and on small game, though their hunting rights had been drastically curtailed by Interior Department conservation measures. Curtis went on to tell Leupp that, though he had not visited the Cañon in person during the summer of 1905, he had heard the same story from several reliable sources, and it really did seem that not more than six of the Cañon's families had enough food to last the winter. 'They need help', he wrote, 'and that quite soon'.

Leupp had been a renowned journalist and an active member of the Indian Rights Association before becoming Theodore Roosevelt's very active Commissioner from 1905 until the end of his mentor's Presidency in 1909. Curtis knew him personally and, while no record of Leupp's reply exists, it is likely that—though he was known to resent the interventions of the Indian Rights Association and other external pressures once he was in office—he did respond to the critical situation facing the Havasupai. If to little avail: by the time the Havasupai section of *The North American Indian* appeared, it was necessary for it to state the facts starkly: 'in 1903 the Havasupai numbered about 250, but in three years disease has diminished their population to 166'.[4]

The second incident involved the President himself. On February 6, 1906, Roosevelt wrote to Curtis to compliment him on his success in securing funds from J. Pierpont Morgan for his North American Indian work: 'I congratulate you with all my heart. That is a mighty fine deed of Mr Morgan's'. Precisely how it came about that the powerful banker and magnate was persuaded to make such a publication possible is not certain. Roosevelt had given his general blessing to the venture in a very fulsome tribute after Curtis had asked him for 'a letter of introduction to Mr Carnegie or anyone else' who might be interested, but in his reply the President had issued a specific ruling: 'there is no man of great wealth with whom I am on sufficiently close terms to warrant my giving a special letter to him'. Since Roosevelt was engaged in major political and economic tussles with several men of 'great wealth' at the time, including Andrew Carnegie and Morgan, doubtless he was *not* in the best position or disposition to seek favours. The financial settlement occurred through the conjunction of a number of factors—the newspaper response to Curtis' exhibitions, for instance, the particular nature of the proposal, and other endorsements of Curtis' work—but the single most effective element was most probably the good offices of Robert Clark Morris, an influential Republican lawyer, leading counsel to the Morgan Bank, and one of Curtis' patrons.[5]

Curtis outlined his project on paper for Morgan's benefit and then, on January 24, 1906, had the favour of a meeting—almost an audience— with the financier. During this meeting—or perhaps in the course of a second one a couple of days later—Curtis had the opportunity to show Morgan some of his pictures; according to Curtis family stories, Morgan, who was of course a major art collector, was so moved by what he saw—including the portrait of 'Mosa' (1903), a young Mohave woman, the lines of whose face painting and beaded necklaces seem subtly to accentuate the wistfulness of her gaze (*illus. 16*)—that he was prepared to become the chief financial backer Curtis had been seeking. In essence, Morgan agreed to finance the fieldwork for the project at the rate of fifteen thousand dollars *per annum* for five years, while Curtis undertook to look after the actual publication himself. The injection of funds from one of the world's richest and most influential men allowed organisational improvements, set a stamp of approval on the project's more ambitious aspects, and gave the Indian work an immediate boost.

Later, in August 1906, emboldened by the grant, by much successful fieldwork, and by a euphoric optimism that was to fuel the project through all kinds of vicissitudes until its completion, Curtis wrote from Hopi country to ask Roosevelt a further favour: 'Could you consider in addition to [my] introduction, an introduction by yourself?' 'It is only the largeness and historical value of the work which gives me the courage to suggest this', he added. 'It is a work of great national worth, during your most active years. Pardon my crude way of saying it, but you as the greatest man in America owe it to your people to do this.' The ebullient President agreed, wrote a laudatory Foreword, and later even signed individual copies of the book's first volume. In 1910, when Curtis told Roosevelt of another major injection of Morgan capital, secured partly through the intercessions of Henry Fairfield Osborn, Director of the American Museum of Natural History, Roosevelt responded, 'Mr Morgan is a trump and Osborn is one of the most useful citizens we have. Your work is a real asset in American achievement'.[6]

On May 27, 1911, in our third incident, Gifford Pinchot, who was then US Chief Forester and later Governor of Pennsylvania, and throughout his career an influential patrician force in American public life, wrote to Curtis with the express purpose of bringing to his attention a newspaper clipping about 'probably the only tribe of really wild Indians left in the United States'. Curtis had been fortunate to secure the acquaintance—indeed, the patronage—of Pinchot many years earlier, even before that of Roosevelt. Their correspondence reveals that Curtis was usually ready to agree with his powerful friend—and a little earlier he had even supported Pinchot against John Muir, another early mentor, in the bitter environmental controversy over the Hetch Hetchy Reservoir. (All three men had participated in the expedition to Alaska led by the railroad tycoon E.H. Harriman in 1899.)

But on this occasion, over the supposedly 'wild' Indians in California, Curtis was sceptical: 'I cannot help but suspect that here is a case where people have let their enthusiasm run away with them'. 'I have been looking into this matter a little since the first newspaper note of it', he continued, 'and I take it that the Indians in question are simply one of the roving bands of Shoshonean stock, which at times are out in the hills, and at other times are, like all the rest of the Indians of that country, hanging about the towns'. 'All of the Indians of that region are given to going back into the hills for the purpose of hunting, and gathering acorns and berries', he explained. 'Of course this little group may be guilty of some special depredation, and for the time being are trying to keep under cover, but I should be surprised if you could not find in the crowd men who could speak English'.[7]

The fourth incident occurred a little later: an exchange of letters between Curtis and Woodrow Wilson's Secretary of the Interior, Franklin K. Lane, in 1915. Lane, a Californian newspaperman and lawyer, was an extremely diligent worker who believed passionately in the need for public officials to take full responsibility for the business of their departments. He thus exhibited a much greater interest in Indian Affairs than most Secretaries of the Interior and imprinted his views on Cato Sells, his Commissioner. He wanted to make maximum use of the national land resources consistent with current conservation policies, and one aspect of this emphasis was a concern to pass over to individual Indians as much responsibility as possible.[8]

Curtis joined one of the Secretary's first-hand investigation parties during the same year as this correspondence and, in general, knew him quite well when he volunteered a response to one of Lane's schemes:

> Since talking with you, I have given a good deal of thought to your plan of establishing organizations with different groups of Indians and I grow more and more convinced that it can be worked out in a satisfactory way and should prove of tremendous value. The principal problem, as I as I see it, will be to get satisfactory local men to assist in establishing the plan. In order to get the subject fixed in my own mind, I tried to figure out its application in certain places. To do this I figuratively placed myself as the one in charge of the Crows and asked the question, 'What would I do to bring out the best in these people'? and the answer was, 'Lane's plan of a modified fraternal organization with a definite plan of reward of merit for accomplishment'.

Curtis did have particularly close ties to the Crow Reservation, and he often visited it. In 1909 the Bureau had sought his advice on improving medical services there and, in general, he probably did envisage himself well-qualified to represent the Crows as 'the one in charge'.[9]

The proposal at issue—'Lane's plan' to awaken greater Indian interest in the responsibilities of quasi-citizenship through participation in fraternal organisations akin to those so popular among whites at the time (the Elks, the Kiwanis, etc.)—was one strand in a network of efforts to speed up the process by which individual Indians could cease to be the responsibility of the Bureau and their lands become part of the general agricultural economy of the West and the nation at large. An aspect of fraternal organisations which was actually introduced to the Indian context was the initiation ceremony. Lane himself, who in another exchange of letters with Curtis expressed an interest in traditional Plains initiation rites, such as the Sioux Foster Parent Chant, supervised the first of the 'Last-Arrow' ceremonies at the Yankton Sioux Reservation in 1916, in which Indians were encouraged to shoot a symbolic last arrow before donning (white) 'citizens' dress' and accepting US citizenship.[10]

In an additional paragraph in his letter to Lane about fraternal organisations and the Crows, Curtis disparaged both the Progressive senator from Wisconsin, Robert La Follette, a long-serving member of the Senate Indian Affairs Committee who was often seen as a champion of Indian rights, and Helen Pierce Grey, who from 1908 onwards had made a number of allegations about Bureau mismanagement of Crow affairs. 'If Senator La Follette is still furthering the destructive activities of Helen Pierce Gray [sic], please urge him to drop the matter and give you a chance to handle the situation,' Curtis admonished. 'What the Crows need the most at this time, is freedom of agitators'. Later the same year, Indian Inspector James McLaughlin told Curtis, 'the Secretary . . . is a great admirer of yours', and asked for his views on 'the enfranchisement of a certain class of Indians . . . whose competency in transacting their business affairs justifies conferring full citizenship upon them'. While there is no record of Curtis' response, many whites were enthusiastic, and on April 17, 1917, with much fanfare, Cato Sells duly declared 'the dawn of a new era'.[11]

The new policy for Indian affairs—which would be more accurately described as the acceleration of implementation of an existing policy—had as its primary element an effort to change the status of as many individual Indians as possible from that of 'half ward and half citizen' to that of citizen. This was to be done by issuing of certificates of 'competence' to all educated Indians, and to as many others as could be deemed able to conduct their own business, especially with reference to the disposal of their lands, in the white world. Sales of land were to be made easier, at the discretion of the owner, and many more Indians, especially full-bloods, were to become US citizens. Needless to say, the new policy also witnessed the speedier transfer of a vast acreage of land from Indian to white hands.

There was always a tension, usually unacknowledged, between various of the Bureau's declared roles and objectives. The potential for Indian self-determination implied in the acceleration of the granting of certificates of competence, for example, was at the same time *denied* by both the Bureau's claim to guardianship of the true interests of Indians and its actual absolute authority on each reservation. By the nineteen

Edward S. Curtis' Indian Photographs

as yet no ready acknowledgement anywhere in the white community
that the status granted to Indians was in effect that of colonial subjects,
there was increasing awareness of Indian claims to cultural and religious
freedom. There were, indeed, many more 'agitators' in the field,
including the writer Mary Austin, who was particularly concerned about
the Indian Office's efforts to suppress traditional Pueblo ceremonies,
sometimes on the grounds of their supposed 'indecency'. The Indian
Defense Association, under the energetic leadership of John Collier—
later Franklin Delano Roosevelt's long term Commissioner—had superseded the Indian Rights Association as the premier white pressure group
and was beginning to promote policies that, if adopted, could lead to a
hedged form of cultural pluralism. It advocated tribal landholding,
self-government through tribal councils, religious freedom, the creation
of organisations to promote the sale of traditional crafts, and a complete overhaul of the education, health and water supply services for
Indians.[12]

This was the context for returning to what constitutes the fifth and
final incident: Curtis' lecture at the new anthropological museum in
Santa Fé in July 1924. In that the predominant preoccupation of the
North American Indian project was traditional lifeways, in Curtis'
phrase, 'the old time Indian', it might be expected that he would have
favoured the more culturally pluralist approaches of the Indian Defense
Association, but in fact, as I will elaborate, he opposed them. In 1923
he helped to found the Indian Welfare League. The other leading figures
were Marah Ellis Ryan, a popular romantic novelist; Dr John Adams
Comstock, Director of the Southwest Museum in Los Angeles; and,
most prominently, Ida May Adams, a Los Angeles attorney. Others
associated with the League were the lawyer William Jennings Bryan Jr,
the cowboy movie star William S. Hart, and Harry C. James, then a
young volunteer worker on the Hopi reservation collecting evidence of
abuses by a particular agent there. Unlike the Indian Defense Association, the Indian Welfare League—as its name implied—worked primarily as a charitable organisation for Indians—finding work, providing
legal services, and raising funds. But, increasingly, as one of its reports
makes clear, pressure group activities, especially lobbying on Capitol
Hill, came to the fore. The single most significant achievement for which
it claimed credit (a credit ironically unrecorded in the relevant historical
literature), was the successful passage of the Indian Citizenship Act of
April, 1924, the piece of legislation which extended US citizenship to
all Indians.[13]

The bulk of Curtis' speech concerned various white attitudes and activities that he believed were harmful to Indians, but it began with a disquisition on 'the greatest weakness'—not of whites, but of Indians. This 'weakness', as Curtis thought, was 'self pity':

> The Indian as a whole from North to South, from East to West, in this year of 1924 is the star sob-sister of the Universe. He spends a great part of his time weeping on his own shoulder. Self pity is absolutely fatal to the individual or to the Community. It is worse than dope. We as people are very much given to encouraging them in this self pity. We listen to their tales of woe and we agree with them that they have been robbed of everything—most of them have—and that we are going to help them in all their problems.

Having seemingly doused in his audience all sympathy for Indians, as if such sympathy were indeed incendiary, Curtis went on to discuss 'the Indian's greatest burden': 'his white friends, the amateur and professional "mussers" '. He concentrated on the professionals—'call them propagandists, call them whatever you like'—and, whatever their motives, lumped them all together as 'assisting Indians for selfish purposes only'. Some of them, he said (possibly with D. H. Lawrence in mind), were 'writers going upon reservations . . . in search of original material . . . [which, for effect, had to be] something sensational.' The remainder of the lecture recounted the activities of such persons in a series of anecdotes.

One such figure, unnamed (but probably Helen Pierce Grey), had allegedly incited a northern Plains tribe to physical violence to prevent her own justifiable arrest by Indian Department police. Another, Jonathan Tibbets, had apparently appropriated for himself dues paid into his Cooperative Indian Organization by 20,000 Southern California Indians. A third figure, also unnamed, a 'professional fixer' based in Northern California, had allegedly collected dues from 8000 Indians and was in the process of 'binding all the Indians into a six year's contract to pay him' at an annual rate of three to six dollars, with the promise that he would 'recover . . . all of the lands they had lost under the old original treaties,' which, as Curtis put it, was 'absolutely impossible'.[14]

Finally, again without naming anyone, but with New Mexico and the defence of ceremonial practices in view—and presumably, with leaders like Mary Austin and Collier in mind—Curtis laid down a distinction 'between religious practice and wrongdoing': 'as long as a man carries on his religious beliefs and wrongs no one, well and good,—but if he commits a wrong in the name of religion, it does not right that wrong'. By placing this anecdote in the same series as the others, which, if true, were about obviously 'criminal' types, Curtis was deeply disparaging to people who considered themselves—and were considered by others—as reformers. It was a position Curtis developed at greater length in another speech or article of this same period titled 'The Indian and his Religious Freedom', in which he claimed that certain ceremonies were 'obscene' and that traditional religious leaders exerted dictatorial powers which infringed the individual rights of certain members of the tribe, thus humiliating them.[15] In essence, of course, while seeming to embody empirical commonsense, such a distinction—between religious beliefs and wrongdoing—works very much against notions of cultural pluralism in that it reserves to the speaker, and to the speaker's (white) society, the sole authority to decide that which is 'right' and 'wrong', as if the referents of these constituted universal transcendent values.

Each of these incidents deserves to be high-lighted or shaded in by its own detailed cross-hatching of annotation, of course, but considerations of space allow only for the broader brush strokes of general commentary. First, the degree to which Curtis shared the position of 'the Department', 'the Office', is very obvious; even some of the denigratory vocabulary of the 1924 lecture—'professional mussers' and 'agitators'—was commonly adopted by the Bureau and its apologists at the time. In the case of Leupp in particular their positions may have been even closer than the exchange over the Havasupai alone would indicate. Leupp took seriously a set of suggestions Curtis submitted about Red Cloud's people on the Pine Ridge Sioux Reservation in South Dakota. With much attention to specifics, Curtis advocated that in the then pending allotment process at Pine Ridge, a series of contractual obligations should be set in place whereby Indians would guarantee that they—and others they would sign for—would use wisely and profitably such seed potato, grain, breeding stock, and the like that they received, and that they should be rewarded with further such distributions when they did so, and penalised when they did not.

When Leupp received Curtis' letter, in August, 1905, he added a note: 'Here's something for the wiseheads of the Office to chew on. Please report on it to me with reasons pro and con'. While the appointed anonymous Bureau 'wisehead' was mostly 'con'—he seemed to think the actual procedures could work, but that Indians would not understand the idea of a 'contract'—Leupp himself was very much a supporter of the notion that Indians should be made individually independent, both of the tribe and the government, and this was the emphasis of his first, 1905, Annual Report. In 1906, his report stressed how Indians would be forced to earn their living by paid labour—even if it meant compelling them to leave the reservation in search of work. Indeed, in speaking particularly of Pine Ridge, he gave an account of local efforts there to remove Indians from the rations roll and to get them into an employment bureau. It is clear that the details of Curtis' proposal, the idea of a kind of contract with individual Indians, was not put into practice at Pine Ridge or anywhere else, but the generalities of such views must have struck a chord.[16]

Lane, too, had an ear for Curtis. In a letter of April 13, 1915, he told him, 'It is good to have the support of those who have lived close to the Indian and who have some real conception of the problem', and though Curtis was out in the field when Lane asked his views on granting more Indians the 'competence' to conduct their own business affairs, there is every reason to believe he would have endorsed this form of selective assimilation.[17] In the 1924 lecture Curtis insisted that problems and abuses on Indian land should be taken to 'the Department'—which, within the limitations of its own red tape, would, he claimed, always make a serious effort to find solutions—whereas discussing them with Indians themselves would only foment unnecessary aggravations. In saying such things in 1924, in the face of the broadening of the spectrum of influential white opinion that we have already observed, Curtis seems to have held close to an Indian Office line which, if only temporarily, was itself becoming more entrenched. And it was a convergence of view that was too close to be explained solely by the project's need to seek favours and patronage.

Roosevelt's remark that Curtis' work was 'a real asset in American achievement'—made, incidentally, when Morgan's largess enabled the establishment of The North American Indian, Incorporated—can, I think, be better understood. If for the time being we leave aside the irony which should be obvious to a present day reader—in that, generally speaking, an 'American achievement' so often entailed a Native American *loss*, even destruction—there was in 1910 a sense in which the project's reflection of political attitudes towards Indians made it so entirely typical that it was actually appropriate to describe it as an 'American achievement'. In *The West as America* William H. Truettner, following Richard Slotkin, has stressed the existence in western expansion of 'a controlling entrepreneurial group', pointing out that 'most "pioneers" were prompted to act by the marketing policies of the nearest metropolis', and that the very 'existence of a metropolitan-based expansion system clarifies the relationship between patrons, artists, and [their] images'. Truettner has argued that artistic observation of the West occurred essentially in association with, even from the point of view of, 'those who stood to gain most from the westward movement—the leaders of the industrial East'. If granted, this means that, far from being depictions of the 'true West' that they have so often been described as, such images have functioned as ideology; they were such powerful embodiments of prevailing myths of the West that they have conferred upon their subject matter what Truettner has called 'a quality of absolute legitimacy', as if 'what is being described is natural and unquestionable and, therefore a fully sanctioned enterprise'.[18]

While Truettner's comments were addressed mainly to paintings, they apply equally well to photographs. And Curtis, with the then richest man in the world as his chief patron, and his other primary subscribers encompassing not only government figures like Pinchot but also railroad entrepreneurs such as E. H. Harriman, bankers with western investments, men with western mining and property interests, and numerous others who were undoubtedly members of 'a controlling entrepreneurial group', must be seen in this context. The North American Indian project did not follow a rigid ideological line, but it is precisely the self-contradictory nature of some of its pronouncements that tend, in themselves, to disclose the presence of such an ideology. The fundamental issue of the 'vanishing', the 'passing' or demise of Indians, reveals this most tellingly. With reference to the Havasupai, for example, *The North American Indian* gave no sense that they had suffered a major catastrophe, the worst effects of which might have been averted, and instead ascribed their decrease in numbers by over a third in just three years to the wholly natural cause of 'illness'.

Similarly, with reference to Pine Ridge, the Introduction to volume three of *The North American Indian*, which was published only a couple of years after Curtis communicated his ideas on guarantees to Leupp, contained no such notions, did not mention that Curtis himself had witnessed Pine Ridge people literally starving as a result of the non-arrival of food rations supposedly guaranteed by treaty obligations, and even fatalistically ascribed the problems of the Sioux only to 'the fact that they are Indians, and lack by many ages that which is necessary to enable them to meet the competition of the Caucasian race'. Also, the exchange with Pinchot has a coda: while, in the absence of the particular news story at issue between them we cannot even determine the likely specific Indian people concerned, we can be sure that Curtis would have been utterly confounded in his scepticism by the appearance a few months later, in Oroville, California, of Ishi, hailed repeatedly as 'the last wild man in America'. Ishi, the final surviving member of the Yahi tribe, wandered into the (appropriate) environs of a slaughterhouse on

August 29, 1911, and ended his days living in the anthropological museum at Berkeley, where he demonstrated aspects of Yahi traditional life.[19]

Perhaps it is not surprising that Curtis' conclusions to his 1924 speech were shot through with ambiguities, even with downright contradictions. On the one hand, in advocating that problems on Indian land should be taken to 'the Department' rather than be discussed with Indians themselves, he appears to have believed that Indians were not capable of making up their own minds, let alone taking decisions and acting. On the other hand, in arguing against the preservers of traditional ceremonies and customs, he was categorically assertive: 'an Indian cannot be a museum specimen. Nor can he be an exhibit in a zoological park'. Rather, as he put it, 'they must take their place with advancing civilizations, alongside the white race. They must solve their own problems as we have, otherwise, they perish'. From *this* perspective, Indians would *have* to think and act for themselves. Finally, despite the previous demand for Indian advance 'alongside of the white race', Curtis cautioned, 'we must not expect too much . . . The change must come very slowly . . .'

This tangle of attitudes, as I have indicated, was by no means unique to Curtis. He himself may have genuinely believed that he was bringing new thinking to bear on 'the Indian problem' during these exchanges— and it may appear that in one of them the Bureau 'wisehead' was conducting a kind of unacknowledged dialogue with him, as if his position was quite separate from the Bureau's—in fact the views he articulated were very much within the parameters of assumptions dominant at the time. Because the 1924 ones were expressed in the abbreviated form of a speech, the tangle may have been somewhat knottier than its appearances elsewhere, but several historians have shown that the same strands ran through the dominant society as a whole. Indeed, it was precisely the benumbing confusion in the un-relenting and confident battery of decisions and dicta to which Indians were subjected over a long period that helped to create the sense of dependency and powerlessness that has still to be set aside completely.[20]

The ideological imperatives we have outlined were expressed in visual terms by Curtis, sometimes attended by the same sense of contradiction. In 1924, the same year as the Santa Fé lecture, he made an image of a semi-naked Indian woman standing among the fan-like foliage of one of the thick palm groves of Palm Cañon, California, to which he gave the title 'Before the White Man Came' (*illus. 17*). Such a photograph, so captioned, is, of course, a conceptual if not an optical illusion. While purporting to render *Indian* life before the advent of white people, its existence and essence were totally determined by white, Euro-American culture. It was created with an instrument of that culture, the camera, and, more important, it was visualised according to the norms of that culture, both in its adherence to the rules of perspective of that culture and in its long-established generic conventions: the grove is edenic and the as yet unashamed Eve awaits her fate. Similarly, when Curtis' Indian figures were depicted as lone and heroic 'noble savages', possibly even intended to expiate wrongs perpetrated on Native American peoples, they were nevertheless—as Truettner said of Indian figures in paintings by Thomas Cole and Asher Durand—'consigned to a romantic doom that left viewers untroubled' *(illus. 18)*.[21] Truly, however beautiful as imagery, they were not so much *just* 'traditional' and rooted in the landscape, pushed into the past, as caught in stasis, *removed* from time and its passage altogether.

NOTES

1. Edward S. Curtis *The North American Indian* ed., Frederick Webb Hodge (Cambridge, MA and Norwood, CT, 1907–1930); hereafter NAI. A photocopy of the speech, headed 'New Museum—Santa Fe, July 27, 1924', was kindly provided from the typescript in his possession by Manford E. Magnusson, Curtis' son-in-law, after an interview in April, 1977. Subsequent lecture quotations are from the same source.

2. Information on the North American Indian project—as supplemented by research in primary documents—from Florence Curtis Graybill and Victor Boesen, *Edward Sheriff Curtis: Visions of a Vanishing Race* (New York, 1976); Bill Holm and George I. Quimby, *Edward S. Curtis in the Land of the War Canoes* (Seattle, 1980); Christopher M. Lyman, *The Vanishing Race and Other Illusions: Photographs of Indians by Edward S. Curtis* (Washington, DC, 1982); Barbara A. Davis, *Edward S. Curtis: The Life and Times of a Shadow Catcher* (San Francisco, 1985).

3. These comments are necessarily an abbreviated, oversimple view of a complex phase of Native American history. Fuller accounts can be found in volume two of Francis Paul Prucha, *The Great Father: The United States Government and the American Indians* (Lincoln, NB and London, 1984) and Frederick E. Hoxie, *A Final Promise: The Campaign to Assimilate the Indians, 1880-1920* (Cambridge and New York, 1989). A succinct account is provided in two successive chapters of Wilcomb E. Washburn, ed., *History of Indian-White Relations* (Washington DC, 1988), pp. 51-81, the fourth volume of the *Handbook of North American Indians*.

4. Curtis to Leupp, October 17, 1905, Letters to Commissioner, Record Group

75, National Archives. NAI, II (1908), pp. 95-9; also reprinted in M. Gidley, ed., *The Vanishing Race: Selections from E.S. Curtis' The North American Indian* (Seattle, pb. ed., 1987), pp. 30-1.

5. Roosevelt to Curtis, February 6, 1906 and December 16, 1905, Theodore Roosevelt Papers, Library of Congress. Cf the accounts too numerous to cite which claim erroneously that Roosevelt introduced Curtis to Morgan. Further information on Morris, Morgan and related matters will be included in Mick Gidley, *Edward S. Curtis and The North American Indian, Incorporated* (forthcoming).

6. Curtis to Roosevelt, August 17, 1906, and Roosevelt to Curtis, February 27, 1910, Roosevelt Papers.

7. Pinchot to Curtis, May 25 and Curtis to Pinchot, May 27, 1911, Gifford Pinchot Papers, Library of Congress.

8. Brief commentary on Lane may be found in Prucha, *The Great Father*, II, pp. 770 and 879.

9. Curtis to Lane, April 12, 1915, Major James McLaughlin Papers, Assumption College, Richardton, North Dakota; Father Louis Pfaller kindly searched the papers for Curtis letters. Data on Curtis' relations with the Crows appears in the book by Gidley cited in note 5. For medical advice, see Acting Commissioner F.H. Abbott to Curtis, November 6, 1909, Crow File 96051-1909, Record Group 75.

10. See Curtis to Lane, May 15, 1915, McLaughlin. Material on the Last Arrow ceremonies may be found in Hoxie, pp. 180-1.

11. In general, there was much dispute over Indian Office abuses on the Crow Reservation; see, for example, Prucha, II, p. 774. In hearings of the Congressional and Senate Committee on Indian Affairs, April 1-13, 1908, Mrs Grey made several charges of maladministration on the Crow Reservation; see the report of the hearings, 'A Company for breeding horses on the Crow Reservation . . . and on bill S2963, for surveying and allotment of Indian lands', issued by the Government Printing Office, 1908. McLaughlin to Curtis, June 23, 1915, McLaughlin. The 'declaration' was reprinted in Sells' Annual Report of 1917; extracted in Wilcomb E. Washburn, ed., *The American Indian and the United States: A Documentary History* (Westport, CT, 1973), Vol. II, pp. 867-9.

12. For more detailed historical contextualisation than can be provided here, see Randolph C. Downes, 'A Crusade for Indian Reform, 1922–1934', *Mississippi Valley Historical Review*, 32 (1945), pp. 331-45; Kenneth Philp, *John Collier's Crusade for Indian Reform, 1920–1954* (Tucson, 1977), especially chapters two to five; and William G. Robbins, 'Herbert Hoover Indian Reformers Under Attack: The Failures of Administrative Reform', in Carl E. Krog and William R. Tanner, eds., *Herbert Hoover and the Republican Era: A Reconsideration* (Lanham, MD, 1984), pp. 95-119.

13. Information on the League seems very sparse and was found through scattered, mainly Los Angeles, newspaper references, interviews with Curtis family members, *Who's Who in America*, other general sources, and Harry

C. James, *Pages from Hopi History* (Tucson, 1974), pp. 180-1, 190. Most important was a pamphlet kindly supplied by Stephany Eger of the Museum of New Mexico titled 'Activities of the Indian Welfare League' (c.1924), which includes an account of the citizenship struggle. The League goes unmentioned even in Gary C. Stein, 'The Indian Citizenship Act of 1924', *New Mexico Historical Review*, 47 (1972), pp. 257-74.

14. Unfortunately, it has not proved possible to unravel the intricacies of any of these cases, but some light on the Southern California situation was shed by Sells in one of his reports; see Washburn, ed.,*The America Indian and the United States*, II, pp. 899-902.

15. Curtis, 'The Indian and his Religious Freedom', typescript in NAI materials at the Los Angeles County Museum of Natural History. In a manner too involved to be summarised here this item should be seen as a riposte to a pamphlet by John Collier with virtually the same title; see Philp, pp. 55-70.

16. Curtis to Leupp, August 14, 1905, with note by Leupp and response, Letters to Commissioner. Leupp's Annual Reports for 1905 and 1906 were reprinted in extract form in Washburn, ed., *The American Indian and the United States*, pp. 735-46 and 751-3, respectively. For a concise account of Leupp's policies, see Donald Parman's essay on him in Robert M. Kvasnicka and Herman J. Viola, eds., *The Commissioners of Indian Affairs, 1824-1977* (Lincoln, NE and London, 1979), pp. 221-32.

17. Lane to Curtis, April 13, 1915, and Lewis Albert to James Mclaughlin, June 24, 1915, Mclaughlin.

18. William H. Truettner, *The West as America: Reinterpreting Images of the Frontier, 1820–1920* (Washington, DC and London, 1990), especially pp. 38-53.

19. NAI, III (1908), p.xii. Information on the physical condition of the Pine Ridge people from an interview with Harold P. Curtis, Curtis' son, for whom it was a vivid memory, in February 1977; Curtis told Leupp that Red Cloud's people had 'got into' his brain, and this may have been why. See Theodora Kroeber, *Ishi in Two Worlds: A Biography of the Last Wild Indian in America* rep. ed. (Berkeley, Los Angeles and London, 1976).

20. See works cited by Prucha, Hoxie and Philp; see also Robert Berkhofer, *The White Man's Indian: Images of the American Indian from Columbus to the Present* (New York, 1979), especially pp. 166-97; and Brian W. Dippie, *The Vanishing American: White Attitudes and US Indian Policy* (Middletown, CT, 1982).

21. Truettner, p.43. See also Mick Gidley, 'The Repeated Return of the Vanishing Indian', in Brian Holden Reid and John White, eds., *American Studies: Essays in Honour of Marcus Cunliffe* (London, 1991), pp. 189-209.

RICHARD MALTBY

John Ford and the Indians; or, Tom Doniphon's History Lesson

'No-one goes to the Western for a history lesson.'

Kevin Brownlow[1]

There is a moment, not quite at the climax of John Ford's *Two Rode Together* (1961), in which the contradictions of Hollywood's representation of the American Indian are encapsulated. It is a woodland night on a studio set; the lawman/Indian trader hero sits with the woman he has ransomed back from Comanche captivity. To the crashing accompaniment of Indian drums, brass and strings, the chief, villainously resplendent in eagle-feather war-bonnet and brandishing a knife, bursts into the circle of light around the camp-fire. He embodies the magnificent, threatening, ignoble animal of savagism, his intentions violence, rapine and despoilation. Calmly, belying the dramatic potential of the confrontation, the hero shoots him.

In this archetypal confrontation between savage Indian and frontiersman over the fate of feminine civilisation, we witness a paradox: the divergence between the terrifying image of the Indian and his actual impotence in the sights of the white hero's gun. The Threat vanishes as soon as it becomes visible. This encapsulates a condition of the Western: the Indian constitutes an immediate physical threat to the hero and his charges, yet he cannot but be vanquished, wiped out by the vanguard of civilisation. However, little in this particular archetype is pure: its details of characterisation and casting make it carry undercurrents of every racial tension in American history. The white man's motivations are mercenary and cynical, the woman is Mexican and the Indian is personified by a black man, Woody Strode. We lack only an immigrant to complete the cultural capsule, and Ford himself performs that function: 'Who better than an Irishman could understand the Indians, while still being stirred by the tales of the U.S. Cavalry? We were on both sides of the epic'. Ford's comment, made during the production of his last Western, *Cheyenne Autumn* (1964) is echoed in that film by Sergeant Wichowsky, played by Mike Mazurki as a revised version of the Victor McLaglen character in Ford's cavalry trilogy. Wichowsky expresses the Indians' plight in the terms of a white history:

> I'm a Pole. You know what they have in Poland besides Poles. Cossacks. You know what a Cossack is? A Cossack is a man on a horse with a fur cap on his head and a sabre in his hand. Now he kills Poles just because they're Poles, like we're trying to kill Indians just because they're Indians. I was proud to be an American soldier. But I ain't proud to be a Cossack.[2]

Ford's Indians, then, are to be understood in terms of one or other white historical paradigm, but whoever these Polish-Irish characters impersonated by Caucasians, Latin- or African-Americans are supposed to be, it is evident that they make no attempt adequately to represent the tribal nations whose names they appropriate. In the Hollywood Western there are no 'real' 'Indians'—no Iroquois, no Lakota, no Navajo, only Hollywood Indians with different names. With hardly an exception throughout its history, the Hollywood Western has obliterated the ethnic and cultural distinctions between the many indigenous peoples of North America, and imposed on them a stereotype, itself derived from the earlier traditions of the dime novel, the historical romance, and the captivity narrative.[3]

The Hollywood Indian represents an Other defined in relation to white American experience. It seems almost too banal to mention, but as an account of Native American culture, *Two Rode Together*, is, quite typically for the Hollywood Western, irredeemable, worse than worthless. Near the end of the film, Elena de la Madriaga (Linda Cristal) and Guthrie McCabe (James Stewart) describe the gendered division of labour among the Comanche to a group of Army officers and their wives:

> Elena: For five years I was the woman of the Comanche Stone Calf. He treated me like a wife. The work was hard, the scoldings frequent, and occasionally he beat me. I did not bear him any children. . . . I know that many of you regard me as a degraded woman, degraded by the touch of a savage Comanche, by having had to live as one of them.
> McCabe: . . . The Comanche, he don't know when Sunday comes. And cooking's sort of the recreation for their women. And then in their spare time they chew the glue out of buffalo hides so that their men can have a nice soft pair of mocassins. Well, you can judge for yourself what kind of a life it is by the number of survivors we brought back.

From such ethnology we can learn only a white story; that is, a story of white fears, desires and neuroses, in which are inscribed the three dominant terms of the Western mythos, the Three Rs of the Western: Racism, Rape and Repression. The act of representation is here an act of appropriation, a racism undertaken, according to Jack Nachbar, 'for purposes of creating mythic narrative'. It is often difficult to tell what white male writers mean when they deploy the term 'myth' in such contexts. Jon Tuska is suitably scathing: '[W]hat apologists really mean by a "mythic" dimension in a Western film is that part of it which they know to be a lie but which, for whatever reason, they still wish to embrace'. The Western is, as Douglas Pye says, 'at root a triumphalist white genre', its white triumphalism its ideological purpose, its remorseless racism deeply embedded in its structures, long predating the movies themselves.[4]

The logic appears to be that to invoke the Western is to plead what amounts to a mythic version of the First Amendment—the right to rewrite history in the name of free mythopoeia. At the same time, the myth is 'really about' something else, something determined by external historical forces. By this formulation the myth is left with no specific content. A 'mythic' Western, not content just to be itself, must busy itself with themes and subject matter. Critical interpretation of the postwar Western, the Western André Bazin called the Superwestern, 'a Western that would be ashamed to be just itself, and looks for some additional interest to justify its existence—an aesthetic, sociological, moral, psychological, political or erotic interest', has made much of the idea that the Western and its signs, and the Sign of the Indian in particular, are highly mutable, open for transfer to a variety of other contexts. Brian Henderson, for instance, suggests that:

> The emotional impact of *The Searchers* [directed by Ford in 1956].
> can hardly come from the issue of the kinship status and marriage-
> ability of an Indian in white society in 1956. . . . It becomes
> explicable only if we substitute black for red and read a film about
> red-white relations in 1868–1873 as a film about black-white
> relations in 1956.

Henderson is employing a common critical strategy, one in part designed to elevate the text's status by way of demonstrating its 'relevance'. The supposition that Indians in post-war Westerns 'stand for' some other, more contemporary figure has its source in a limited application of idea of myth and allegory, which looks to attach a monosemic, one-to-one connection between symbol and symbolised. The movie only pretends to be a Western. 'For instance', announce William T. Pilkington and

Don Graham quite blithely, 'in the late 1960s and early 1970s many Westerns . . . were not about the old West at all; they were really about the American involvement in Vietnam'. Philip French practices a more evasive piece of critical legerdemain in arguing that: 'from around 1950 the Indian in the contemporary allegory can stand for the Negro when the implications are social or for the Communist when the implications are political, though generally the identification is somewhat woolly'. Indeed. But where does the woolliness in this process lie? By such critical devices the Indian becomes simply an empty signifier of the Other in search of a conveniently relevant signified. At its most innocent, this idea of mutability is an attempt to explain the durability of the Western myth through its capacity to adapt to changing cultural conditions. The weakness of this practice is that the critic may attach the moveable symbol of the Indian where and when s/he pleases. Now 'standing in' for this, now for that, the Hollywood Indian is, by this conundrum, never himself. Such criticism denies him whatever identity Hollywood has not already removed, and reinforces the Western genre's intense structural racism.[5]

In an essay on *Ulzana's Raid*, Jack Nachbar comments on the intense self-referentiality of the Western:

> Each time we participate in a cavalry charge, a stage holdup, a cattle stampede we relive the golden moment of the American past when civilization and frontier stood toe to toe . . . To recreate over and over this romanticized American history on screen requires, quite obviously, immense shortcuts in exposition and development. Audiences are shown images that immediately suggest broad patterns of historical meaning.

Protestations such as this, frequently making generalised claims about the 'importance' of the Western are numerous in the body of Western criticism, but there is among them a curious reluctance to discuss what substance the Western as myth has. In an expression of consensus opinion on the affirmatory role of the Western in American culture, Ray Allen Billington suggests that the frontier myth expresses the individualism and 'back-to-Nature urge' which is part of the persistent American rebellion against a conformist urban industrial society. This begins to approach the function of myth more seriously, but Billington's pastoral idyll addresses neither the genre's racism nor its appropriation of history. In *Sixguns and Society*, Will Wright borrows the methodology of structuralist anthropology to suggest that the mythologies of modern societies,

establish an analogy between past and present in the same way
that primitive myths establish an analogy between nature and
culture. . . . The Western, and all such historical myths, describe
the past in terms of the present . . . Myth reproduces the conditions
and concern of the present in the past . . . Through images that
mean more than they seem to, historical myths illustrate how the
conflicts of the present were successfully resolved in history.[6]

The Western is several things at once—a myth of origin, an adolescent
male fantasy, an account of the individual's relation to society, and more.
It is seldom only one of these things, particularly in its twentieth century
version, where the accretions of significance make it excessively mean-
ingful. The Western is a myth written in such condensed script that its
images and events are charged with a multiplicity of available meanings.
So far from being a simple shoot-'em-up, the Western is massively
overdetermined with multiple significances. Its prevalence in American
culture is the result of this overdetermination, and of the Western's
capacity to represent across several fields of American experience, while
retaining the same structure. It is written by and written in the
assumptions of American culture; they are not so much its subject as its
speech. It may, perhaps, even be that one reason that American culture
tells itself the Western story over and over again is to try to convince
itself that its evasion of contradiction will pass as a resolution.[7]

On the frontier between civilisation and savagery, the Western hero
is necessarily in a contradictory position, but a Western does not have
to engage the contradiction. Many Westerns, perhaps particularly
children's stories, act as a kind of bank for storing the Western's
metaphorical structure for future circulation. Even in such a bank,
however, they accumulate interest in the form of additional significations
through the way that contradictions are not engaged. Devices such as
disguise and casting permit the evasion of uncomfortable contradictions,
while the twinned commercial properties of the disposability and
repetition of serial fiction provide overwhelming incentives for that
evasion. In dime novels, B-Westerns and TV series, the hero rides
into the sunset at story's end so that he can ride out of the sunrise
at the same time next week. So long as this permits an appropriate
amount of performance and spectacle in the text for it to deliver its
pleasures to its audience, the self-regenerative quality of this fiction does
not require the contradictions to be resolved. The Western myth is a
commodity form; the hero is a function of its commercial existence as
well as its morphology. We may read the imagery of the sunset (so clichéd
that we do not need it—heroes ride into the sunset whether there is a

sunset or not) as a conventional sign of death. But, of course, we do not need to.

★

'This is the West, sir. When the legend becomes fact, print the legend.' Maxwell Scott, editor of the *Shinbone Star*, in *The Man Who Shot Liberty Valance*

This is Tom Doniphon's History Lesson: the inevitable confusion of history and myth in the Western. It is announced by Maxwell Scott (Carleton Young), the newspaper editor to whom Ransom Stoddard (James Stewart) has just told his revisionist history of *The Man Who Shot Liberty Valance*. *The Man Who Shot Liberty Valance* is, in legend, Ransom Stoddard, the lawyer civiliser of the West and archetypal embodiment of Ford's populist dream, the bringer of the Book of Law who can uphold it with the gun, a figure who occupies a place in clear line of descent from Ford's Henry Fonda in *My Darling Clementine* and *Young Mr. Lincoln*—and, for that matter, from Edward Ellis' *Seth Jones* (1860).[8] In the 'true story', *The Man Who Shot Liberty Valance* is Tom Doniphon, physical archetype of the Western hero (John Wayne), but too much tainted by the wilderness to resist the descent into anarchic violence and alcoholic degeneracy on the loss of his girl, the Cactus Rose Hallie (Vera Miles), to Stoddard. These two characters represent polar alternatives for the hero's fate, Senator or scapegoat, the lawyer hero of legend which has become history, or the Vanishing hero of a revisionist history which is, of course, myth.

'When the legend becomes fact, print the legend'. We should recognise that Editor Scott does not construct a binary opposition out of his two terms; he is no kind of structuralist. 'Legend' can become 'fact,' and still be recorded as 'legend'. We learn that the 'legend' of the Easterner who learns Western ways and ends up more skilful than the Western bad man misrepresents events. Instead, we witness a 'legend' of Western hero and Western badman/outlaw in symbiotic relationship, in which the deadly encounter between them is ultimately fatal to both. The John Wayne legend becomes 'fact' by being enacted in *The Man Who Shot Liberty Valance*, as the James Stewart legend is held to have become fact by Editor Scott. Ford presents us with both myth and history and explains their relationship. As in *My Darling Clementine*, we are presented with the ideological construct that is the West of legend/mythology, and told that it is history. But in *The Man Who Shot Liberty Valance* we are also presented with the process by which legend becomes fact, history becomes myth and ideology is constructed. This essay proposes a similar strategy to that of Editor Scott. It presumes that the 'legend' of Western expansion has become the 'fact' of the various print and film texts that it takes as its source material. Those texts themselves have a history, but they also contain an idea of History, and of the West as History, which is itself 'legend' rather than 'fact'—mythology. The subject of my enquiry is mythology rather than history; to be more precise, it is the history of a mythology which masquerades as History but, like the Senator, knows itself to be lying.

The legend becoming fact is a description of the process of history being written, for Ford and for empiricist historians alike, although of the two Ford might well feel happier with the definition. In this, Ford follows tradition. The Western is always a story of Vanishing Americans. The frontier is always closing, having encountered History and retreated West. By the time we get to tell stories about the frontier, it has gone. The frontier was inscribed as History into fiction almost at the moment of its happening, and that inscription involved a recognition that what was being inscribed had passed. Wayne Sarf offers two versions of a similar story:

> In 1849 the famous mountain man and guide Kit Carson . . . had an odd experience when he sought to free a white woman held captive by some Apaches, who, however, killed her and escaped: in their camp Carson found a paperback novel, its cover showing him rescuing a fair maiden from fiendish red men. In one possibly apocryphal tale, Carson, shown a journal cover that had him protecting a terrified female while dead Indians littered the surrounding countryside, is quoted as remarking: 'That there might be true but I hain't got no reckerlection of it.'[9]

Implicit in Sarf's remark that one anecdote is 'possibly apocryphal' is an idea that history is inherently verifiable, authentic. But Western history—and particularly the Western history of 1860-1890 that has become the dominant subject-matter of Westerns—has been constructed as a form of mythology, which is not susceptible to rules of evidence. On the localised scale of event, the fictional account of the gunfight at the OK Corral, for instance, existed as a piece of public cultural property *before* the historically accurate version of those events was written. The corrective, revisionist history can never be free of the legend because historically the only consequential element in those events is their legendary status. The formulation of the myth of the frontier preceded the events which would provide its content, and the ideological framework of the myth governed the choice of material for Western history. Then the procedures of narrative fiction operated on the now legendary events to transform them into the material of Western myth, which wrote itself as History, and identified the time of its occurrence as a moment of Vanishment. The legend is inescapable. The History exists because the legend exists. The history of the West is in a sense a subgenre of the Western, and revisionist history a subgenre of that.

In what follows, I want to treat Ford's films as typical instances of a generic discourse, rather than exceptional cases to be revered for their merits or their internal coherence. The auteurist approach to Hollywood has taken Ford as its archetype, and his Westerns are on the whole the most highly regarded of his films, the paradigms used by auteurists to explain such apparent abberations as *Donovan's Reef*. Within the canons of film criticism, Monument Valley came to 'represent' the landscape of the West, encouraging by the extremes of its appearance a view of Westerns as abstracted and allegorical. Because of the Western's paradigmatic status in genre theory, students taking introductory courses with titles like 'Auteur and Genre: Two Critical Approaches to Hollywood' discover, year after year, that the Western is where Hollywood discusses American History, in which the wilderness becomes a garden, and that the Western looks like *Stagecoach* or *My Darling Clementine* or *The Searchers*. Ford has acquired an institutional status in the critical historiography of the Western comparable only to that of James Fenimore Cooper.

Despite critical claims to the contrary, there is little 'original' in Ford's synthesis, but this observation should not be understood as denigratory. The point of comparing *The Searchers* to *Nick of the Woods*, or *The Man Who Shot Liberty Valance* to 'The Big Bear of Arkansaw' is not to counter acclamation of Ford's creative originality or canonic vision, or to suggest derivations, but to examine the persistence of archetypes and discursive frameworks in an attempt to interrogate the kind of cultural discourse that takes place within the Western's framework. Variation and modulation have long been all that is possible in the Western, and to worry about originality is to display a profound misunderstanding of the workings of the genre or of myth. Every Western is a palimpsest, a manuscript written on the pages of an earlier, now partially erased, book, carrying traces of its previous inscriptions.

John Ford's work is permeated with a sense of History, existing both as an external force on the films' narrative and within the films as an agency of motivation for his characters. *Wagonmaster* begins with a song whose opening line is 'A hundred years have come and gone since 1849'. *She Wore A Yellow Ribbon* begins with the impact of the news of Custer's defeat at Little Big Horn—the event fictionalised in *Fort Apache*. In talking about *My Darling Clementine*, Ford insisted on the historical accuracy of his depiction of the gunfight at the OK Corral, claiming conversations with Wyatt Earp as his primary source. Placing his films in history is not, however, limited to this external referencing. In describing the process of writing *Fort Apache*, Frank Nugent relates that Ford made him produce a biography for every character in the picture, accounting for what had brought him or her to the point where they enter the story.

> He gave me a list of about 50 books to read—memoirs, novels, anything about the period. Later he sent me down into the Old Apache country to nose around, get the smell and feel of the land. When I got back, Ford asked if I thought I had enough research. I said yes. 'Good', he said. 'Now just forget everything you've read and we'll start writing a movie'.[10]

The process of learning and forgetting which Nugent describes is recurrent in Ford's films, to be understood as part of the revision of history, 'printing the legend'. The most conspicuous device by which it is introduced is through Ford's graveside scenes. In *She Wore a Yellow Ribbon* the personal history of Captain Nathan Brittles and the military history of Custer's Last Stand are tied together through reminiscence at the graveside of his wife Mary: 'We had some sad news today, Mary. George Custer was killed, with his whole command. Miles Keogh. You remember Miles, happy-go-lucky Irishman, who used to waltz so well with you. Yeah, I know, I guess I was a little jealous. I never could waltz myself'. Ford's films are consciously retrospective, in that a sense of the past as an active force in the present, is ingrained in them. The films, too, reverberate among themselves, echoing each other in ways of which we and they are always at least half-conscious. There is, for example, a remarkable consistency in the characters John Wayne plays: Tom Doniphon is a tragic version of the Ringo Kid, and both of them, like Ethan Edwards, Kirby York and Nathan Brittles, are excluded from history.

Ford spoke of his last Western, *Cheyenne Autumn*, as an apologia to the Indians:

> I had wanted to make it for a long time. I've killed more Indians than Custer, Beecher and Chivington put together, and people in Europe always want to know about the Indians. There are two sides to every story, but I wanted to show their point of view for a change.[11]

In *Cheyenne Autumn* motifs from previous films, particularly *She Wore A Yellow Ribbon*, are transferred from whites to Indians. Ben Johnson's escape from Indian pursuit in that film is repeated across the same scenery by an Indian escaping from whites. Only the screen direction is reversed. Where, in *She Wore A Yellow Ribbon*, the Seventh Cavalry are consigned 'only a cold page in the history books to mark their passage', in *Cheyenne Autumn* the Cheyennes' trek is described as 'a footnote in history'. More significantly to Ford's rhetoric is the sense in which the Chief's funeral echoes 'Trooper Clay's'. In *Cheyenne Autumn* the values inherent in these motifs are transferred wholesale from their previous location in the small Western community or the Cavalry to the Indians. In the process Ford provides a new critique of white Western figures in James Stewart's gambling, knockabout version of Wyatt Earp, and of white motivations, when a newspaper editor tells his staff,

> In the *Sun*, *Times*, *Chronicle*, take your pick, they're all saying the same thing we're saying, burning, killing, violating beautiful white women. It's not news any more. We're going to take a different tack. From now on, we're going to grieve for the noble Redman. We'll sell more papers that way.

But the depiction of the Cheyenne remains couched firmly in the rhetoric of Ford's previous communities, and is mediated through the film's white stars: Richard Widmark, Carroll Baker, Mike Mazurki, and Edward G. Robinson playing Secretary of the Interior Carl Schurz, who celebrates the end of the Cheyennes' trek by offering them cigars in place of their empty peace-pipes, in effect reproducing the image of the cigar-store Indian.

★

Learning and forgetting, making legend fact, are as much part of the critical history of the Western genre as they are part of the genre's work. The notion of the Western as heroic events set in a time which has just passed into legend, of the West as an era which is ending or has just ended, is something which has also been passed on to the Western itself. Almost never in its history has the demise of the Western *not* been predicted. That demise, however, might more appropriately be seen as a displaced acknowledgment that the cultural contradictions implicit in the Western narrative are not susceptible to resolution. A reductive version of the twentieth century myth would suggest that the Western triangle, of Indian, Westerner and woman—of savagery, heroism and civilisation—is shaped so that the hero has to interpose himself between the other two terms, conventionally to save the woman from the corruption of a fate worse than death, less frequently to protect the

Indian from what Doc Boone, in the last line of *Stagecoach*, calls 'the blessings of civilisation'. As codified by James Fenimore Cooper, this narrative might be summarised as: 'The hero goes outside civilisation to protect it from savagery. He does not return'.

Cooper's centrality to the development of Western mythology comes from the originality of his synthesis in the *Leatherstocking Tales*, in which the frontiersman ceases to be merely the guide and comic acolyte of the light hero of romance, and becomes the dramatic central protagonist in the novel romantic form of tragic optimism or optimistic tragedy. In Cooper's version of the myth the minor, peripheral characters are saved to continue their optimistic work of natural destruction by the tragic death of the American hero, the 'Saint of the woods'. However noble he may be, Leatherstocking is made to recognise over and over again that he may never settle in the settlements he has made possible, and thus, like the Indian who is his companion and his enemy, he is driven ever westward, in dread of the end of the frontier. The inheritor of Indian skills, he is the Indian's nemesis and he shares the Indian's destiny as America's most popular tragic hero. Although Leatherstocking never doubts the incompatibility of the two cultures, part of his contradiction is that the scout is nevertheless a 'medium . . . a link between them [the Indians] and civilized life', explaining each to the other.[12] It is, centrally, in the contradictions constructed around the frontiersman hero, the Indian fighter as cultural broker, the hunter who explains what he kills to those for whom he kills it, that the rich overdeterminations of the Western have been able to flourish. For while such contradictions cannot be resolved within the narrative, they provide opportunities for inflecting a given plot either to a comic celebration of the entry into marriage, or to a tragic meditation upon the cost of such optimistic outcome.

One cultural function of the post-Civil War Western was to provide a meeting ground for Southern codes of chivalry and Northern, commercial versions of Manifest Destiny. The optimistic version of this encounter was the transcendent Western hero whom Robert Warshow eulogises in his essay on the Westerner as 'the last gentleman', personified in Owen Wister's *The Virginian*, the civiliser who lives by the code of the West and settles down to run his ranch with his Eastern schoolmarm bride. In the tragic account, however, the white Southerner is a scapegoat hero. Having refused either to surrender or to resign his allegiance to the Confederate States of America at the end of the Civil War, Ethan Edwards is the Western hero as displaced Southerner, in search of a new site for his racist anxieties. The Comanches who have captured his niece represent only one of the places towards which he could direct the misanthropic intensity of his racial hatred. 'Our racial prejudice and our guilt for it', says Brian Henderson, 'are placed on his shoulders, then he is criticised, excluded, or lampooned, mythically purging us of them . . . Ethan is excluded for our sins; that is why we find it so moving'. Henderson perceives *The Searchers* as offering a liberal commentary on white/black relations, but in order to achieve the necessary structural parallelism to make his case, he finds it necessary to propose that the secondary hero of the film, Martin Pawley (Jeffrey Hunter), who is one-eighth Cherokee, functions 'in the unconscious symbolics of the film as pure Indian'. The 'unconscious symbolics', therefore, equate with the overt racism of Ethan Edwards, the hero, whose horror of miscegenation casts him in the mould of Leatherstocking, the 'man without a cross' in his blood. As Henderson points out, Ethan's concern for racial purity is inconsistent; he seems unconcerned by either of Martin's prospective marriages, to Look (Beuhlah Archuletta) or Laurie Jorgensen (Vera Miles), to Indian or white.[13] One might hypothesise a number of options from Ethan's inconsistency; that his concern is exclusively with family, from which he repeatedly excludes Martin; that, despite his superficial racist aggression to Martin, he in fact regards him as white and therefore a suitable marriage partner for Laurie, while having no more objection to Martin's taking a squaw than Generals Crook or Custer had to their soldiers raping Indian women; or that, perhaps, Martin's one-eighth Cherokee blood was on the female side, and therefore culturally acceptable.

Ethan Edwards is Ford's most rabid Indian-Hater, and it is a commonplace in critical discussion of *The Searchers* that Chief Scar is Ethan's dark, libidinous id. Throughout the film, they are closely paralleled. Ethan's arrival at the farm precedes Scar's by a day; Scar seeks revenge for the death of his two sons, while Ethan seeks revenge for his lost family. If Scar is the despoiler of the family, the home and centre of ritual in Ford, Ethan, too, disrupts ceremonies—Laurie's wedding, and, in a different sense, the home ceremonies of Martha and Aaron (Walter Coy). He more violently disrupts Ford's most sacred ceremony, the funeral, not once, but twice. Ethan and Scar are locked in combat over the possession of women, Martha (Dorothy Jordan) and Debbie (Natalie Wood): the Indian enacts what is, by force of social taboo, proscribed to the white man. Their combat is timeless: time passes in *The Searchers* without being accounted for. The story covers perhaps seven years, but only Debbie, to whom the passing of time means the threat of sexual maturity, grows any older.

Critical recognition of the parallel in *The Searchers* between white hero and Indian villain derives from responses to Ethan's psychological extremism. When similar attitudes to his are expressed by the eminently balanced Guthrie McCabe in *Two Rode Together* neither Quanah Parker (like Scar, played by Henry Brandon) nor Stone Calf are widely identifed as 'unseen, ungovernable forces of the libido'. Racism in this movie appears as a social convention, institutionalised and quite acceptable. As a civil rights allegory *Two Rode Together* reads poorly; it asks for sympathy and cultural acceptance only for the white women who have been tainted by Indian life, not for the Indians. But when Elena describes to McCabe how whites look at her,

> These people . . . their eyes are all on my body, like dirty fingers, as if they would turn their backs I would leap upon them and my touch would have to be washed off like filth. . . . Now I see the silent questions. How many braves has she known? How many mestiso children carry her blood in their veins? Why didn't I kill myself when I took a Comanche?

—his response is to force her into an embrace and kiss her. Elena is the impossible object, the unsullied victim of atrocity. The transparency of her skin, her perfect teeth, the conventions of Hollywood's presentation of female beauty as object of the male gaze, belie her and McCabe's description of life among the Comanche. For the audience, her spiritual virtue shines out of her physical appearance. But the other characters, bound by restrictions of plot and convention, perceive the survival of her beauty quite differently, as itself a sign of her degradation. The female survivors of Ford's captivity narratives are dark women, physically unmarked by their ordeal, unlike their fair counterparts. To survive as a woman in the wilderness, to be degraded and yet unblemished, is to embody a contradiction in patriarchy's construction of true womanhood, to indicate, perhaps, a forbidden desire. The return of the captive woman now lacking a proper social place is precisely the Return of the Repressed. Of no worth and highly valued, an object of pity and of desire, Elena generates McCabe's libidinous desire because she has no property value, because having already been degraded and rendered valueless she cannot be further defiled. The sign of Elena's beauty must be understood in its ambiguity, as the sign of Hollywood's capacity to represent but not to resolve contradiction. The white woman who has 'lived as one of them', become 'Comanch', now embodies the appeal, as Richard Slotkin phrases it, of 'the forbidden, the beautiful-horrible "other"' . . . an alternative world and culture, erotically and socially freer than our own, antithetical to and an escape from the civilisation that both sustains and discomforts us.'[14] *Two Rode Together* makes no attempt to resolve these contradictions. They are merely stated, and ended by a conclusion that imposes gratuitous romance on frontier tragedy. Such a device displays all of Hollywood's usual opportunism, further evidence of the fruitlessness of a search for consistency or formal coherence in the Hollywood text.

Women, whose structural function is to elevate men to a higher plane of civilisation, can themselves be reduced to a lower plane by the consequences of capture. The Western's division of heroines into light and dark—schoolmarm and saloon-girl—is rigorously maintained by the movies. The dark heroine is doomed by her knowledge of the hero's sexuality, but the fair, for instance the blonde white women captives in *The Searchers*, can be degraded out of their skin colour into a self-perpetuating Otherness. When the sergeant of their guard comments, 'It's hard to believe they're white', Ethan Edwards is insistent: 'They ain't white—any more. They're Comanch'. When Ethan finds that Debbie has become Scar's woman, he disowns her, making a new will declaring that he is 'without any blood kin'. The white woman 'defiled' by Indians has lost her property rights along with her property value.

Two Rode Together sustains an economic metaphor, in which women and Indians are regarded as property, and the characters who so regard them are disapproved for doing so. When McCabe explains to Marty (Shirley Jones) what her brother would now be like (correctly, in terms of the film's representations of Indians), he goes beyond describing his appearance to tell her, 'given the chance, sister, he'd rape you . . . and when he'd finished he'd trade you off to one of the other bucks for a good knife or a bad rifle'. Quanah Parker engages in exactly such trade, of people for guns and knives, with McCabe. Elena knows that 'Stone Calf will never let me go', because she is property, but, like the other 'debased' women in the Indian camp, she believes 'I am not worth fighting for'. Like Henry J. Wringle (Willis Bouchey), McCabe finds that hunting for captives interferes with business, so he attempts to turn his errand into the wilderness into a business venture. During his exchange with Major Forsyth (John McIntire), he reveals his plans to rescue captives for money. The Major demands, 'Just how much do you think human lives are worth, McCabe'? 'Whatever the market will bear, no more, no less', he replies. Leaving the young male captive he plans to sell to Wringle with Jim Geary (Richard Widmark), he tells him, 'Keep an eye on Junior, Jim. You know he's worth a thousand bucks to me'—an uncomfortable, if ignored, double entendre. But Wringle rejects his goods: 'You couldn't pay me to take in a mad dog like that'. When

McCabe protests about the boy's being claimed by another family, Geary insists, 'You heard Henry J. He wouldn't take him as a gift'.

In Hollywood, Love conquers economics: Marty, like Jim, is unconcerned about the Army's low pay. Those who would make people property receive their comeuppance: Stone Calf is killed; Belle (Annelle Hayes), who has proposed marriage by offering McCabe 50% instead of the 10% he gets as Marshall, and who tells Elena 'Everything around here belongs to me, including the livestock', loses McCabe to Elena. McCabe's desire restores Elena's knowledge of her true value as the capitalist contradiction, the property which is without price. But that contradictory process of valuation which is the containment of greed can be understood only in terms of the movie's running economic metaphor: Jim's last line to Belle, as McCabe and Elena depart for California, is 'I guess old Guth finally found something he wanted more than 10% of'. Having bought Elena from Quanah Parker, McCabe discovers a value outside the bourgeois processes of valuation, and invests it in the property called woman.

Women in the Western represent civilisation because they represent property values. Savages are a threat to be exterminated because they do not respect or acknowledge the value of property. Naturally, they direct this lack of respect against civilisation's most cherished symbol of property, woman. The white woman's symbolic role as the embodiment of the civilisation which will destroy the wilderness and replace the frontier is not a position of power. As the bearer of children, civilisation, progress and history, she may represent an inevitable abstract force, but as an individual she is vulnerable to degradation—the fate worse than death from which Hatfield (John Carradine) aims to save Mrs. Mallory (Louise Platt) with his last bullet in *Stagecoach*. Brian Henderson says:

> Scar's crimes—rape, murder, dismemberment, burning—eminently violate the law that dictates postponement of pleasure. His acts stand in for the terrifying libido that must be repressed and, if unrepressed, must be punished drastically. His crimes 'stand in' for libido because, of course, libido cannot be represented.

The Indian Other has done what may not be done, and may not be admitted to have been desired, and may not be shown. The majority of Western narratives, even in the postwar period, have retained the tradition of coy discretion in describing the fate worse than death, leaving the audience to 'fill in the blanks', to invent what, in *The Searchers*, Ethan Edwards and the movie 'thought it best to keep from you'.

Henderson notes the effect this device has in requiring the viewer to project fantasies onto the film, and thus to identify with the violation and also the need to punish it. This process, which gives pleasure by exercising libido and ego reassurance by suppressing it, imaginatively reconstitutes the structure of the self, thereby promoting what has been called 'the maintenance of the subject'.[15]

★

'Racist, me? My best friends are blacks: Woody Strode and my servant, who's lived with me for thirty years'. John Ford[16]

The year before he made *Two Rode Together*, Ford made *Sergeant Rutledge*, also with Woody Strode, who plays the eponymous central character, the 'top soldier' of a Ninth Cavalry unit accused of the murder of his commanding officer and the rape-murder of his sixteen-year-old daughter. At the climax of the courtroom drama around which the film is structured, it is revealed that the actual killer is the post storekeeper (Fred Libby), driven by uncontrollable desire: 'I had to, I had to! Don't you understand? She—the way she walked, the way her body moved. She drove me crazy! I had to have her, I had to, I had to. Oh, God help me, God help me'. If Elena's account of 'the eyes on my body' sparks McCabe's desire, the beginning of *Sergeant Rutledge* inverts the pattern to repeat the threat in *The Searchers*. Fair Mary Beecher (Constance Towers) is confronted with the savage threat—first Strode, then Strode's warning of the Indians—immediately after she has been violently seized and kissed by Tom (Jeffrey Hunter), the white officer hero. On each occasion, the 'provoking' of white male desire is linked to the Indian sexual threat. Ethan's psychopathic performance permits the schizophrenic/symbiotic relation between frontiersman hero and Indian villain to be rendered explicit, but the patterns described in *The Searchers* are reproduced, less emphatically, in *Stagecoach*, *My Darling Clementine*, *Two Rode Together*, and *The Man Who Shot Liberty Valance*.

In *Sergeant Rutledge*, which deals overtly with white racist representations of blacks—with 'the myth of the black rapist'—the Indians are as stereotyped as in *Stagecoach*.[17] Strode plays Rutledge as a figure who instills into his men a belief that 'We're fighting to make us proud'; 'some day', he says, the Buffalo Soldier will have achieved sufficient dignity and pride to be accepted by whites as 'a man' and not 'a swamprunnin' nigger'. The struggle to achieve this entry into white history understood as progress is a battle waged against the Indian, who is represented entirely without sympathetic consideration in *Sergeant Rutledge*. In the attack on the railroad station, Strode gives Mary his revolver, saying, 'You're a Western woman, you can use a gun. They'll have no mercy on you, lady, they'll have no mercy'. In the river ambush, we see the Indians blending into the landscape, hiding in the tall grass by the banks, and when they attack, seeming to 'spring up out of the earth'—the words Mary uses to describe her first encounter with Rutledge, 'like a nightmare'.

Rutledge's task, throughout the film, is to overcome the plot's first sight of him: a naked dark arm, grasping the mouth of a terrified white woman—we do not immediately know if the hand is black or red. He must overcome this impression, and the stereotyping of him as a raping, murdering savage, by demonstrating his difference from the raping, murdering savages who are in the movie. Rutledge's right to a place in history is asserted by his disciplined military prowess, demonstrated most spectacularly by his skill in killing Indians. The old Sergeant Skidmore explains to Mary Beecher (the invocation of Harriet Beecher Stowe in her name seems hardly incidental) that a 'soldier can't never think by his heart, ma'am, he's got to think by the book'. Rutledge shows that he has absorbed the 'the book' of Law, Regulation, and the postponement of gratification, in the moment when, rather than make his escape, 'something kept telling me I had to go back'. The black soldier demonstrates his innocence of the symbolic burden of the white man's guilt and repressed desire by his possession of that white Puritan virtue, the inner voice that postpones pleasure. In *The Searchers* the Indian can 'stand for' the black when the black is himself an undeclared symbol of repressed white male desire, but when blacks are themselves represented in a conflict over that symbolism, the Indian has no function beyond the occupation of the extreme point of Otherness. Woody Strode's role in *Two Rode Together* is quite incompatible with his role in *Sergeant Rutledge*. In *Two Rode Together*, Strode is the raping murdering savage that he is not in *Sergeant Rutledge*: the black actor playing the Indian playing the white man's libido is different from the black actor playing the black character trying to demonstrate that he is not symbolic of the white man's libido. Who is disguised as whom? Which of these is the Vanishing American with whom, according to Leslie Fiedler, the white boy first essays manhood?[18] And who, for that matter, is concealed behind a white man such as Henry Brandon (Quanah Parker in *Two Rode Together*, Chief Scar in *The Searchers*) 'playing' 'Indian'?

There are precursors for Woody Strode's embodiment of the Child of Darkness in *Two Rode Together*. In William Gilmore Simms' *The Yemassee* (1835), one of the minor characters defies the Indians who are about to torture him: 'Ay, ye miserable red nagers,—ye don't frighten Teddy Macnamara now so aisily'. In Robert Montgomery Bird's *Nick of the Woods* (1837), Colonel Tom Bruce, commander of the station, talks of killing 'two of the red niggurs' in revenge for Major Forrester's death. Fiedler suggests that, in *Huckleberry Finn*, Twain 'turned his Negro protagonist into a Noble Savage, ie. an Indian in blackface,' and notes Cooper's use, on the title page of *The Last of the Mohicans*, of Othello's line, 'Mislike me not for my complexion' as an instance of what he calls 'the mythological adaptation . . . of the Negro character to the myth of the Indian'. Caliban, he argues, contains within himself an anticipatory history of both Red and Black American destinies. Described as both 'a savage and [a] deformed slave', he is the victim of Prospero's expropriation and his attempts to 'civilise' him. For having tried to rape the white man's daughter, he is enslaved. With the white renegades, who introduce him to liquor, he stages an unsuccessful revolt.[19]

The Party-goers at Boston disguised themselves as Indians. The question we must ask is not so much whether white culture has sought to represent indigenous people accurately or not, as what aspect of itself it has understood them to represent. In the confrontation between savagery and civilisation which is at the heart of frontier myth, the 'Indian' has been cast as the savage. But our recognition of the function 'Indian/savage' cannot be restricted to persons of an appropriate skin colour or make-up. On the nineteenth century stage and throughout Hollywood history white actors and actresses have taken the speaking parts in 'speaking for the Indian'. But if the Indian is a creature of white mythology, played by whites who disguise themselves as savages in order to behave savagely, then it is an arbitrary confirmation of a racist definition of difference to presume that the 'savage' function in the Western myth is only represented by white performers in 'Indian' costume. Savagery must be a more mobile function than such a limited prescription suggests.

From the Puritans Western mythology adopted the practice of displacing their forbidden desires onto people they called savages, so that 'the extermination of the Indian became a cleansing of those sins from their own midsts as well as the destruction of a feared enemy'. The purpose of the errand into the wilderness was to return unsullied. Captivity and hunter narratives alike present the encounter with the wilderness as an act of regression into a primal world where the Children of Light must combat the Children of Darkness. Robert Berkhofer writes,

If they can maintain their racial/cultural integrity in that world, and if they can defeat the forces that seek to prevent their return to civilization, then on their return they will be capable of renewing the moral and physical powers of the society they originally left.

But the entry into the wilderness was a regression, and its danger and its temptation lay in the possibility of being mastered by the wilderness rather than mastering it. Implicit in the idea of regression was the notion that the wilderness had the power to turn the civilised savage. For Puritan captives both their chastity and their souls were at issue. The hunter, 'who learns from the Indians only in order to destroy them and so make the woods safe for the white woman', risks descending into savagery himself. As one character declares in *Nick of the Woods*, 'd-n me; for I'm a white Injun, and there's nothing more despisable'.[20]

This is Leatherstocking's dilemma. With his incessant proclamation that he is 'a man without a cross', Cooper's hero, more than any other character, insists on his own racial purity. That purity also ensures his chastity, the force that motivates Western heroism, displacing sexuality into violence and guaranteeing a resolution in blood. Cooper kills his dark heroine, Cora of the tainted blood, desired by Uncas and Magua alike, rather than permit the forbidden act of dark seduction. Even though she is already, in her father's words, 'degraded' by her mother's ancestry, the deaths of all the novel's dark characters do not offer the possibility of compromise or integration. When, at the funeral of Cora and Uncas, Colonel Munro asks Hawkeye to tell the Lenape that 'the time shall not be distant when we may assemble around His throne without distinction of sex, or rank, or colour', the scout replies, 'To tell them this . . . would be to tell them that the snows come not in the winter, or that the sun shines fiercest when the trees are stripped of their leaves'.[21]

But if the hero may not legitimately commune with the Other, he can easily disguise himself as one of them, as Martin, by taking off his shirt and throwing a blanket over his shoulder, does in *The Searchers*. The white man, and particularly the Indian Hater, may become an Indian at his convenience. In *Nick of the Woods*, 'Wrapping his blanket about his shoulders, and assuming the gait of a savage, [Nathan] stalked boldly forwards . . . relying on his disguise as all-sufficient to avert suspicion'. There is inevitably a degree of equivocation in this cultural cross-dressing, a desire to escape the burden of one or other restricted, conventional role, most strongly in the desire to escape the repressions of Whiteness. Throughout the dime novel it also serves as a convenient device to cover over a central contradiction in Western narrative: the incompatibility of East and West within the conventional structures of romance. From Oliver Effingham's masquerade as Edwards in *The Pioneers* (1823), Western heroes have revealed themselves to be Easterners in disguise, genteel enough after all to conclude the romance by leading the heroine to the altar for the conventional wedding. In some dime novels the same process takes place across the sexual divide, when the Indian girl is discovered to be an upper-class white girl captured and educated by the Indians but (like Debbie in *The Searchers*) fundamentally unchanged: 'beneath the savage costume she was almost as genteel as ever'.[22]

Disguise permits the unification of separate identities, and separate narrative functions, within a single character. In literature, with whatever facility it is employed, it *is* a facile device. For the movies, disguise is more complex. The audience must see through the disguise to maintain the security of their viewing position and identification; the need for this is most obvious in films involving sexual cross-dressing, but no less legible in the idea of blackface in minstrelsy. At the same time the transparency of disguise opens up the pretense of verisimilitude and cracks the fiction. The movie both does and does not want its audience to believe that Jeff Chandler (in *Broken Arrow*) or Burt Lancaster (in *Apache*) is an Indian. But if the star is always him- or herself, thinly disguised as a character, the lesser luminaries of Hollywood inhabit a more incoherent space, where performances actively conflict with each other. In *Two Rode Together*, Woody Strode plays Magua to Stewart's Hawkeye and Widmark's Duncan Hayward; in *Sergeant Rutledge* he plays Uncas/Hawkeye to Jeffrey Hunter's Duncan; in *The Man Who Shot Liberty Valance* he plays Chingachgook to Wayne's Uncas. A peripheral character in *The Man Who Shot Liberty Valance*, Strode's Pompey is nevertheless the accumulated embodiment of so much racial antagonism. He presents us with all the contradictions that are the Other's lot. He is, as the Other always is, an overdetermined sign disguised as an empty signifier.

There are no Indians in *The Man Who Shot Liberty Valance*. That is, there are no white performers 'playing Indian'. But there is savagery in another, white guise. As whites kill the Indian, that part of the white represented by 'the Indian' is not disposed of but left to find a new host. To perform heroic deeds, the Indian-Hater needs the Indian; the lawman, similarly, needs the outlaw. The outlaw has learnt his wilderness lessons from Magua, not Chingachgook. But he knows, and is part of, the civilisation he is in rebellion against, and he is aware of a notion of law which he is outside. The Indian and the outlaw represent savagery on either side of the frontier's 'ideal boundary', one beyond the outer limit of civilisation in the forest, the other just within it, at the edge of civilisation itself.[23] A less extreme, and chronologically later, savage than the Indian, the outlaw can be paralleled to the hero more easily by virtue of their both being white. Nevertheless, he must behave like a savage. In *My Darling Clementine* the Clantons recognise property but do not respect it: they steal cattle, and Billy steals Doc Holiday's woman, Chihuahua (Linda Darnell). They lack civilisation, in the form of a mother for Old Man (Walter Brennan) and the boys. This is, indeed, a perverse patriarchy where a father whips his sons to teach them the lesson, 'when you pull a gun, kill a man'. More abstractly, in *The Man Who Shot Liberty Valance*, Liberty literally tears up the Book of Law. Later, the outlaw wants to be elected to the territorial convention. (Liberty is the agent of the ranchers who want the range kept open, but they are never seen together, and the movie makes no overt attempt to establish the relationship between large-scale business enterprise and anarchic violence.)

The Stoddards' marriage of East and West shows similar signs of discomfort to that of *The Virginian*, although it is Hallie who is the Westerner, civilised by a man who promises to show her real roses. But the return to Shinbone is motivated by Hallie's unrequited love for Doniphon, signified by the Cactus Rose on his coffin. Stoddard can only do for her what schoolma'ams do for Virginians: incorporate them into history. Stoddard's feminine roleplaying, however—he is teacher, dish-washer, waitress, compromiser—affords him no dignity. In their court-ship, Hallie is more mother than lover, and he neither provides nor expects a sexual response. However superficially successful, his marriage and his career have been barren.

The Man Who Shot Liberty Valance is a bleak version of the Western comedy, a Fordian 'problem film.' It disapproves of its hero because it sees through his disguise and yet it cannot bring itself to believe in the survival of heroic virtue. Doniphon's ranch, like Natty's in *The Pioneers* and Ringo's in *Stagecoach*, is outside the community. But for Hallie, unlike Dallas, it is no longer possible to escape from the 'blessings of civilisation'; Doniphon burns down their future home. In following Natty's advice at the end of *The Prairie*, choosing 'the clearing not the prairie', Hallie has perhaps recognised the imperatives of history, which registers progress in the transition of its heroes from 'the private man with a gun to the public man with a lawbook'.[24] Doniphon's burning of his ranchhouse is a recognition that, like Hannah Clegg in *Two Rode*

Together, he is dead; he does not exist in the records of Shinbone. The Saint of the Woods is a martyr. *The Man Who Shot Liberty Valance* recalls Thomas Bangs Thorpe's 1854 story, 'The Big Bear of Arkansaw', in which the hunter becomes what he hunts. Similarly written at and about a moment when the frontier appeared to have closed, it tells the tale of bear hunter Jim Doggett, who becomes so skillful that he clears all the bears out of Arkansas, and is left with nothing to kill once the last great bear, a quasi-mystical beast, surrenders himself to him.

> Doggett is left with the name of the thing he killed and of the place whose spirit the animal was—he *is* 'The Big Bear of Arkansaw'—but Doggett is also an anachronism, and the last view of him is indeed pathetic: a garrulous, tipsy, backwoodsman booster who vanishes from the steamboat in the night.[25]

At the territorial convention in *The Man Who Shot Liberty Valance*, we see two versions of the West's corruption: one is Doniphon, unshaven, dirty, clumsy, and like Doggett conspicuously in irreparable decline; the other is the rope-twirling cowboy, who would grow up to be and is descended from Roy Rogers, the Lone Ranger, Buffalo Bill—the model of Western show business. Doniphon is, somewhat improbably, in an analogous position of knowledge and comprehension to that of Willy Loman and other liberal tragedians of the postwar period. Possessed of a precisely delineated degree of knowledge about his circumstances and the reasons for his condition of irrelevance, he can nevertheless do nothing to change his circumstances. He tells Stoddard, 'Hallie's your girl now . . . you taught her to read and write. Now give her something to read and write about'. Significantly, this is one scene from which Hallie, the embodiment of the purity of the Western dream, is absent. The cowboy, on the other hand, represents the recuperation of contradictions, the detachment of Western skills and Western narratives from their historical context into a demonstration of pure performance skills. The contradictions which he trivialises and renders childish are resolved in the lie of the legend's triumph when Stoddard is elected, and left bitterly unresolved in Doniphon's vanishment.

NOTES

1. Kevin Brownlow, *The War, The West and the Wilderness* (London, 1979) p.223.
2. John Ford, quoted in Tag Gallagher, *John Ford, The Man and His Films* (Berkeley, 1986) p.341. Sergeant Wichowsky reflects a tradition of

nineteenth-century Eastern European literature, typified by the Polish patriot, Ludwik Powidaj, who wrote an article comparing 'Poles and Indians' shortly after the defeat of the Polish insurrection in 1863. See Ray Allen Billington, *Land of Savagery, Land of Promise: The European Image of the American Frontier in the Nineteenth Century* (New York, 1981) pp.144-9. Billington, however, cites no Irish comparisons.

3. In February 1911, during the American cinema's first cycle of Westerns with Indian characters and themes, the industry trade paper *The Moving Picture World* reported that 'two Chippewa delegations and Indians from other sections have joined in an "uprising" against the moving pictures. They charge that the moving picture promoters, in order to get thrilling pictures of wild western life, have used white men costumed as Indians in depicting scenes that are not true pictures of the Indians, and are in fact grossly libelous.' The paper offered editorial support: 'Truthfulness in pictures has previously been advocated in these columns, and it is well that this timely and authoritative protest should come. While we still have the real Indians with us, why cannot thoroughly representative films be produced, making them at once illustrative and historic recorders of this noble race of people, with their splendid physique and physical powers? It is to be hoped that some of our Western manufacturers will yet produce a series of films of REAL Indian life, doing so with the distinct object in view that they are to be of educational value, both for present and future use. Such a certified series will be of great value'. In practice, however, 'truthfulness' appeared to mean authenticity in costume and avoiding plot clichés. Reviewing Path's *The Unwilling Bride*, directed by James Young-deer, in August 1912, the paper appreciated that, 'There were no burnings, no scalpings; no portrayal of the red man as always bad, the white man as always good. It was a picture that would extract a grunt of satisfaction from the genuine aborigine—and it is a fact that the Indian is a moving picture follower second to none in his steadfastness. *The Unwilling Bride* depicts the Indian as he is understood by those whose knowledge of the red man is gained from sources more authoritative and reliable than the average Indian "drama." . . . To watch [George Gebhart in the leading Indian role] mount and dismount a pony, to see him running—stealthily, catlike, swift—is to open a book of Fenimore Cooper. He is a wonder at Indian portrayal.' *The Moving Picture World*, Vol 8, p.581 (March 18, 1911); p.473 (Mar 4, 1911); Vol 12, p.731 (May 25, 1912); Vol 13, p.434 (August 4, 1912). See also Peter Stanfield, 'The Western 1909-14: A Cast of Villains', *Film History* Vol 1 (1987), pp.97-112.

4. Jack Nachbar, 'Ulzana's Raid', in William T. Pilkington & Don Graham (eds.), *Western Movies* (Albuquerque, 1979) p.140. Jon Tuska, *The American West in Film: Critical Approaches to the Western* (Westport, CT, 1985) p.237. Douglas Pye, 'John Ford and the Critics', *Movie* 22 (1976), p.42.

5. André Bazin, *What is Cinema? Volume II* (Berkeley, 1971) p.151. Brian Henderson, 'The Searchers: An American Dilemma', in Bill Nichols (ed.),

Movies and Methods Volume II (Berkeley, 1985) p.444. William T. Pilkington and Don Graham, 'Introduction', Pilkington and Graham, p.10. Philip French, *Westerns* (London, 1973) p.81.

6. Nachbar, p.140. Billington, p.313. Will Wright, *Sixguns and Society: A Structural Study of the Western* (Berkeley, 1975), pp.208, 211, 212. For a balanced critique of Wright, see Christopher Frayling, 'The American Western and American Society', in Philip Davies and Brian Neve, *Cinema, Politics and Society in America* (Manchester, 1981), pp.136-62.

7. 'Those who do fail to reread are obliged to read the same story everywhere'. Roland Barthes, *S/Z*, trans. Richard Miller (New York, 1974), p.16.

8. Edward Ellis, *Seth Jones; or, the Captives of the Frontier*, published as Beadle's Dime Novels No. 8, 1860.

9. Wayne Michael Sarf, *God Bless You, Buffalo Bill: A Layman's Guide to History and the Western Film* (East Brunswick, 1983), p.253.

10. Lindsay Anderson, *About John Ford* (London, 1981), pp.243-4.

11. Peter Bogdanovich, *John Ford* (London, 1967), p.104.

12. James Fenimore Cooper, *The Last of the Mohicans* (1826; Harmondsworth, 1987), p.347.

13. Owen Wister, *The Virginian: A Horseman of the Plains* (1902; New York, 1979). Henderson, p.447.

14. Joseph McBride and Michael Wilmington, *John Ford* (London, 1974) p.154. Richard Slotkin, *The Fatal Environment: the Myth of the Frontier in the Age of Industrialization, 1800–1890* (Middletown, 1985), p.95.

15. Henderson, p.436.

16. Quoted in Gallagher, p.342.

17. Angela Davis, 'Rape, Racism and the Myth of the Black Rapist', *Women, Race and Class* (London, 1982).

18. Leslie Fiedler, *The Return of the Vanishing American* (London, 1972), p.182.

19. William Gilmore Simms, *The Yemassee, A Romance of Carolina* (1835; New York, 1964), p.270. Robert Montgomery Bird, *Nick of the Woods; or, the Jibbenainosay; a Tale of Kentucky* (1837; New Haven, 1967), p.48. Fiedler, *The Return of the Vanishing American*, p.17 and pp.41-8. Fiedler, *Love and Death in the American Novel* (1960; Harmondsworth, 1984), p.202.

20. Robert F. Berkhofer, Jr., *The White Man's Indian: Images of the American Indian from Columbus to the Present* (New York, 1979), p.27. Slotkin, pp.63, 64. Bird, p.274.

21. Cooper, p.372.

22. Bird, pp.268-9. Kenneth J.M.D. Munden, 'A Contribution to the Psychological Understanding of the Cowboy and His Myth', *American Imago*, 15.2 (Summer 1958), pp.103-48, provides a starting point for consideration of the Western as Oedipal fantasy. See also Leslie Fiedler's argument that the true 'romance in the woods' is the ' "undisturbed and happy intercourse" of the White and Red male friends.' *The Return of the Vanishing American*, p.116. Cooper, as quoted in Henry Nash Smith, *Virgin Land: The American West as Symbol and Myth* (Cambridge, MA, 1950), p.112.

23. Fiedler takes the phrase 'ideal boundary' from Sir Walter Scott's Introduction to *Rob Roy*. *Love and Death in the American Novel*, p.175. See also Smith, p.251.

24. James Fenimore Cooper, *The Prairie* (1827; Harmondsworth, 1987), p.373. Robert B. Ray, *A Certain Tendency of the Hollywood Cinema, 1930–1980* (Princeton, 1985), p.229.

25. Slotkin, p.131.

Notes on Contributors

Anthony Fothergill lectures in English Studies at the University of Exeter, and has also taught at Heidelberg University and Kenyon College, Ohio. His most recent work on Conrad is his book *Heart of Darkness*, published by the Open University Press. He is currently working on *Victorian into Modern*, an edition of critical essays from the period.

Mick Gidley is a Director of AmCAS. He has been awarded grants and fellowships by such bodies as the American Council of Learned Societies and the British Academy; during 1991–2 he held a Fellowship at the Netherlands Institute for Advanced Study, Wassenaar. His publications include several books on Native American themes, a pamphlet titled *American Photography*, essays on American literary topics, and (as co-editor) *Views of American Landscapes* and *Locating the Shakers*. His book on Edward S. Curtis is in final preparation.

Richard Maltby is General Editor of Exeter Studies in American and Commonwealth Arts. He is the author of *Harmless Entertainment: Hollywood and the Ideology of Consensus*, and editor of *Dreams for Sale: Popular Culture in the 20th Century*. He has written extensively on censorship in the American cinema and is currently completing *Reforming the Movies*, a book-length study of Hollywood as a political institution.

Peter Quartermaine has published widely on Commonwealth literature and the visual arts. His study of Thomas Keneally was published recently by Edward Arnold. A Director of AmCAS, he is currently writing a book on the contemporary Australian artist, Brian Seidel.

Stephanie Smiles lives in Exeter and works part-time at the Exeter campus of Polytechnic Southwest. She was born in California and is of Dakota descent. She is currently preparing her doctoral dissertation, 'The European Perception of the Native American, 1750–1850', for publication by Cambridge University Press.

Ronald Tamplin, Senior Lecturer in the School of English and American Studies at Exeter University, is currently Visiting Professor at Université Rennes 2, Haute Bretagne. Poet and critic, his most recent books include studies of T. S. Eliot and Seamus Heaney and *The Arts: A History of Expression in the Twentieth Century*, as editor and contributor. He taught for several years in New Zealand at the Univeristy of Waikato, has travelled widely in the Pacific, written on Pacific themes and has a particular interest in voyage literature and cross-cultural contact in the area.

Tim Youngs is Lecturer in English at Nottingham Polytechnic and the author of several essays on travel writing and colonial discourse. He is married to artist Gurminder Sikand.

Index

Aborigines: 6, 30, 86-8, 91-5
Achebe, Chinua: 9
Adam, Robert: 15-6, 22n4, 23n5
Adams, Ida May: 111
Africa: 5, 25-7, 29-30, 36n9, 45-50, 57, 59n16, 75, 77, 82, 94
Africans: 3, 6-7, 9, 16, 26, 28, 30-33, 40, 45-51, 53, 75, 121
see also specific peoples
Alaska: 108
Alonso, Ana Maria: 9
Anthropological Society of London: 47
anthropology: *see* ethnography
Arens, W.: 59n17
Aristotle: 1
Armstrong, Paul B.: 8, 9, 13n20
Arnold, David: 25, 29
Aruwimi river: 26
Atuana: 69, 72, 75
Aurogard, P.P.: 48
Austin, Mary : 111-2
Australia: 5-7, 30, 80, 84-7, 89-90, 92, 97, 99

Bagamoyo: 26
Barttelot, Edmund: 26, 34-5, 36n15
Bau: 72
Baudelaire, Charles: 49
Bazin, André: 122
Becke, Louis: 60
Becker, Howard S.: 4
Berkhofer, Robert: 137
Billington, Ray Allen: 123, 142n2
Bird, Robert Montgomery: 137
Bora-Bora: 77, 80

Brant, Joseph (Thayendrangegea): 19-20, 24n11
Brassey, Lady: 60-1, 63-5, 67-8, 70-1, 76, 80, 82
Brazil: 37, 58n6, 63
Brennan, Walter: 140
Brisbane: 86
Britain: 5, 15, 26, 45, 99
British East Africa Company: 25
British India Steam Navigation Company: 25
British Museum: 3
Bryan, William Jennings Jr.: 111
Buffalo Bill: 141
Bureau of Indian Affairs: 104-6, 109-10, 113-14, 116
business, business interests: 7, 25, 30, 34, 47, 63-4, 78, 91, 104, 107-10, 112-16, 133-4, 140

Cairns, H. Alan: 46
Canada: 5, 10, 14, 17, 19, 20, 104
canibalism: 37-9, 56-7, 58n6, 59n17, 62, 72
capitalism: see business, business interests
Carnegie, Andrew : 107
Carson, Kit: 126
Carter, Paul: 30
Casati, Gaetano: 29
Chalmers, Rev. James: 98
Chandler, Jeff: 139
Cherokees: 18, 23n9, 131
Cheyenne Autumn: 121, 128-9
Cheyennes: 129
Chippewas: 142n3

Civil War, American: 47, 130
Clarence River Views: 89-90
class, class consciousness: 31, 41-5, 58n8, 60-83, 90, 105, 108
Clifford, James : 3, 11n6
Cole, Thomas: 117
colonialism: *see* imperialism
Collier, John: 111-12
Comanches: 120-121, 130, 132
Comstock, John Adams: 111
Congo: 26, 51
Conrad, Joseph: 5, 9, 12n11, 37, 41-2, 45, 48-51, 53, 56-7
Cook, Captain James: 86
Cooper, James Fenimore: 8, 127, 130, 137-8, 142n3
Cotoner, Nicholas: 16
Cristal, Linda: 121
Crows: 109-10, 118n11
Curtin, Philip: 46
Curtis, Edward S.: 1, 3, 7-8, 103-17

Daggett, R.M.: 6
Darnell, Linda: 140
Darwin, Charles: 6, 47-8, 62, 87
Dawes Act: 105
diary writing: 5, 25-36
drawing, engraving 1, 18, 23n8, 37-41, 90, 92, 98
Durand, Asher: 117

Earp, Wyatt: 128-9
Emin Pasha: 5, 25-6, 29
England: 5, 14-15, 17-19, 22n2, 23n9, 31, 45, 59n8, 65-8, 74, 76-7, 82
Equatoria: 25-6
ethnography and ethnology: 3-4, 18, 26, 38, 42-3, 47, 85-6, 88, 93, 96-9, 104-8, 114-17, 121
Exeter Cathedral: 4, 14
Eyre, John: 90

Fabian, Johannes: 4, 58n6

Fanon, Frantz: 30, 82
Fatuhiva: 73
fiction: 5, 8, 45-57, 97, 112, 125, 127, 130, 136-41
Fiedler, Leslie: 136-7, 143n22
Fiji: 60, 71-2, 74
Fijians: 60, 71-2, 74-5
film: 1, 8, 84, 102n39, 104
    see also western genre
Flaubert, Gustave: 49
Flaxman, John: 4-5, 14-22
Fonda, Henry: 125
Ford, John: 8, 120-2, 125-9, 131-2, 135
Froschauer, Johann: 37
Froude, J.A.: 62, 64
Fussell, Paul: 63

Galton, Francis: 6, 61
Gauguin, Paul: 6
Gibbon, Edward: 78
Gordon, General Charles: 25
Grafton: 86, 88-92, 94, 96
Grand River, Ontario: 19-20
Grey, Helen Pierce: 110, 112, 118n11

Haggard, Rider: 5, 45, 97
Haldimand, General Frederick: 17
Hall, Douglas: 60, 69-71, 73-7, 80, 82
Harriman, E.H.: 108, 115
Hart, William S.: 111
Havasupais: 106-7, 113, 115
Hawaii: 60, 64, 66, 69, 74
Heart of Darkness: 5, 9, 41, 45, 50, 51
Heidelberg School: 94
Helly, Dorothy: 36n9
Henderson, Brian: 122, 131, 134-5
Henley, W.E.: 45
Henty, G.A.: 5
Herodotus: 56
Hetch Hetchy Reservoir: 108

Hollywood: 8, 120, 121, 123, 127, 132-4, 137, 139
Honolulu: 66-7
Hooper, Franklin: 1
Hopis: 108, 111
Huahine: 77, 80

Imperial British East Africa Company: 30
imperialism: 6-7, 15, 17, 20, 25, 30, 34, 40, 45, 47-8, 62, 74, 85-7, 89, 97-9
In Darkest Africa: 27
India: 25, 68, 79, 80
Indians: *see* Native Americans
Indian Days of the Long Ago: 104
Indian Rights Association: 105-7, 111
Indian Welfare League: 104, 111
Iroquois: 18, 121
Irwin, David: 18
Ishi: 115
Ituri forest: 26

Jameson, James: 26, 34, 35, 36n15
Johnson, Colonel Guy; 19, 23n11
Johnson, Sir William: 19, 23n11
Johnstone, H.J.: 87

Kanaka: 73
Kavalli: 26
Kilauea: 68
Kingsley, Dr. George Henry: 60, 76-8, 80, 82
Kingsmill Islanders: 69
Kipling, Rudyard: 5, 45
Klaatsch, H.: 87
Knights of St. John: 16

La Follette, Robert: 110
Lake Albert: 26
Lake Victoria: 59n16
Lakotas: *see* Sioux
Lamary: 39

Lancaster, Burt: 139
landscape, environment: 26, 30, 32, 44, 46-7, 49, 51-3, 58n6, 66, 76, 77, 86-7, 89-90, 92, 95-6, 103, 106, 115-17, 127, 130, 136
Lane, Franklin: 109-10, 114
Lawrence, D.H.: 112
Lenapes: 138
Leopold, King of Belgium: 26
Leupp, Francis E.: 106, 113, 115
Lindt, Johannes: 7, 84-99
Livingstone, David: 36n9, 52, 59n16
London, Jack: 6, 72-3
London Illustrated News: 90
Lone Ranger: 141
Loti, Pierre: 49
Lubbock, Sir John: 33
Lycett, Joseph: 90

Macaulay, Thomas: 78
Mackinnon, William: 25
Maitea: 63
Malta: 16
Man Who Shot Liberty Valance, The: 125, 127, 135, 139-41
Mandeville, John: 39
Manifest Destiny: 130
Maoris: 77, 80, 81
Marquesa Islands: 60, 69-70, 72-3, 75
Marx, Karl: 58n5
Maynard: 95
Mazurki, Mike: 121, 129
McLaglen, Victor: 121
McLaughlin, James: 110
medicine and disease: 5, 27-36, 107, 115
Melanesians: 71
Melbourne: 89, 92, 94-9
Melbourne Argus: 94, 96
Melville, Herman: 60
Mexicans: 3, 10, 120
Mexico: 10
Miles, Vera: 125, 131

Mirambo, King of Unyanyembe: 28
missionaries: 36n9, 46-8, 61, 72-5,
 78-9, 82
Mitchell, W.T.J.: 2
Mohawks: 17, 19-20
Monbuttus: 29
Montaigne, Michel Eyquem de: 37
Morgan, J. Pierpoint: 104, 107-8,
 114, 118n5
Morris, Robert Clark: 107, 118n5
Mountains of the Moon: 26
Muir, John: 108
Museum of Modern Art, New York:
 3
music and dance: 10, 69-71, 76, 80,
 104, 128

Nachbar, Jack: 122, 123
national identity: 7, 84-5, 87-8, 90-1,
 94, 99, 108, 110-11, 114-15,
 120-1, 124
Native Americans: 1, 4-5, 7-8, 10,
 14-22, 37-41, 43, 53, 103-17,
 120-3, 129-40, 142n3
 see also specific peoples.
Navajos: 103, 121
Nerval, Gérard de: 49
New Guinea: 7, 84-5, 89, 92, 96-9
New Mexico: 103, 112
New Review: 45
New South Wales: 88, 90, 92
New Zealand: 60, 63, 81
Ngugi wa Thiong'o: 9
noble savage: 5, 6, 17, 49, 61-82, 87,
 103-4, 117, 142n3
North American Indian, The: 103-4,
 106-7, 111, 114-15
North, Lord: 17
Nugent, Frank: 128

O'Brien, Frederick: 62, 74
O'Brien, Sir George: 74
Orientalism: 2, 11n6
Orwell, George: 61

Osborn, Henry Fairfield: 108
Osborne, Lord Albert: 60-1, 69-71,
 73-7, 80, 82
otherness, concept of: 2, 5, 8-10, 31,
 38-42, 44-6, 49-51, 53-7, 57n5,
 69, 81-2, 85, 90, 97, 121, 132,
 134, 136, 138-40

painting: 3, 6, 10, 15, 19, 23n9, 66,
 75-6, 84-9, 91-3, 114-15, 117
Parke, Thomas: 5, 7, 25-35
Paumotu Islands: 60
Paz, Octavio: 10
Pembroke, George Herbert, Earl of:
 60-1, 76-8, 80-2
Peterson, Nicholas: 93, 96-7
Phillips, Ruth: 10, 13n20
photography: 7-8, 84-119
Picturesque New Guinea: 96-7, 99
Pilger, John: 92
Pinchot, Gifford: 108, 115
Pine Ridge reservation: 113-15
Pioneering in New Guinea: 98
Polynesians: 60-1, 64, 66-7, 71, 75,
 77, 80-2
Pomare, King of Tahiti: 70
Pye, Douglas: 122

Quebec: 17

Raiatea: 80
Raja Sarfogi: 17
Raritonga: 60, 76, 81
realism: 1-2, 7-8, 60, 84-5, 89-90,
 92-4, 96-7, 142n3
Red Cloud: 113
Remington, Frederic: 8
representation, concept of: 1-13,
 38-41, 45, 50, 55-7, 57n5, 81- 2,
 88, 92, 120-1, 128-9, 134, 137,
 139-41
Revolutionary Wars: 16, 19
Reynolds, Sir Joshua: 23n9
Rigaud, Francis: 24n11

Rogers, Roy: 141
Romney, George: 19
Roosevelt, Franklin Delano: 111
Roosevelt, Theodore: 7, 106-7, 108,
    114, 118n5
Rossetti, Christina: 37
Rousseau, Jean-Jacques: 61
Russell, Alexander: 62
Ruwenzori mountains: 26
Ryan, Marah Ellis: 111

Said, Edward: 2, 6, 10-11, 13n20
Saint-Gaudens, Augustus: 7
Samoa: 60, 71, 75-7, 80
San Francisco: 70
Sandwich Islands: 6
Santa Fé: 103, 111, 116
Sartre, Jean-Paul: 82
savage: 33, 37, 39-40, 47, 49, 51, 53,
    59n16, 66-7, 72, 75, 79, 81, 86-7,
    91, 94, 103-4, 108-10, 112,
    115-16, 120, 124, 129, 134, 137,
    139-40, *see also* noble savage
science: 5, 29-30, 33, 47, 84-5, 87-8,
    96
Scotsman, The: 97
Scratchley, Sir Peter: 7, 89, 96
sculpture: 4-5, 14-24, 66-7
Searchers, The: 122, 127, 131, 132,
    133, 134, 135, 136, 138, 139
Sells, Cato: 109-10
Sergeant Rutledge: 135-6, 139
sexuality: 5, 8, 29, 37-9, 51, 53-5,
    71, 77, 80, 98, 121-2, 129, 131-9
Shoshones: 108
Simcoe, Sir John Graves: 4, 5,
    14-20, 22
Simms, William Gilmore: 136
Sioux: 110, 113, 115, 121
Siqueiros: 3, 10
slavery: 16, 36n9, 57n5, 63, 74, 78,
    133, 136-7
Slotkin, Richard: 114, 132
Smith, Bernard: 6

Smith, Henry Nash: 143n22
Social Darwinism: 87
Society Islands: 60, 76-7
Solomon Islands: 74-5
Sontag, Susan: 12n15
South Dakota: 113
South Seas: 3, 6, 60-5, 69-71, 73-5,
    78-9
South Sea Bubbles: 60
Southey, Robert: 58n6
Spender, Stephen: 61
Staden, Hans: 58n6
Stairs, W.G.: 27, 29, 35, 36n15
Stanley, Henry Morgan: 5, 25-7,
    30-1, 34, 52
stereotype, racial: 6, 27-8, 46-8, 50,
    53-4, 56-7, 79, 82, 103, 115,
    121-2, 132, 135-7, 142n3
Stevenson, Robert Louis: 6, 45, 60,
    67
Stewart, James: 121, 125, 129, 139
Stowe, Harriet Beecher: 136
Strode, Woody: 120, 135-6, 139
Sudan: 25
Sunshine and Surf: 60, 69, 75
Sydney: 78, 86, 96
Sydney Morning Herald: 90, 97

Taha: 77
Tahiti: 6, 60, 63, 66, 69-72, 76
Tamatoa, King of Taha: 77
Thackeray, William Makepeace: 71
Thakambau, King of Fiji: 72-3
Thorpe, Thomas Bangs: 141
Thrasymachus: 58n5
Tibbets, Jonathan: 112
Timberlake, Lieutenant Henry: 18
Tippu-Tib: 26, 27
Tonga: 81
Torquay: 65, 69
Townshend, Lieutenant Roger:
    15-16, 20-3
travel writing: 6, 27, 39, 46, 49,
    58n6, 60-83, 98, 112

Trollope, Anthony: 71
Truettner, William H.: 114-15, 117
Tupinambas: 37, 43, 58n6
Tuska, Jon: 122
Twain, Mark : 6, 137
Two Rode Together: 120-1, 132-3, 135-6, 139

United States: 7, 17, 20, 63, 104-5, 108
Unyanyembe: 28

Vespucci, Amerigo: 39
Virgil: 67
Voyage in the Sunbeam, A: 60, 75

Wadelai: 26
Wagner, Conrad: 86
Wanyamwezis: 28
Warshow, Robert: 130
Waugh, Evelyn: 72
Wayne, John: 125-6, 128, 139
Weir, Peter: 84

West, the: 8, 25, 29, 33, 61, 109, 114-15, 125-7, 129, 130, 141
western genre: 8, 103, 111, 117, 120-44
Widmark, Richard: 129, 133, 139
Wilde, Oscar: 44
Williams, Raymond: 34
Wilson, Woodrow: 109
Wister, Owen: 130
Wolfe, General James: 15
women: 5, 6, 27, 29, 31, 51, 53-4, 64-5, 68, 71-2, 80, 107, 116-17, 120-1, 128-9, 131-6, 138-41
Wordsworth, William: 5, 41-4, 51-2, 54, 56
Wright, Will: 123, 143n6

Yahi: 115-16
Yambuya river: 26
Yankton: *see* Sioux
Yeats, W.B.: 61

Zanzibaris: 28-30